"At the start of the COVID-19 pandemic, the Barna Research Group released a startling survey showing more people, some 56%, believe in Satan than they do in God. As troubling as that statistic is, this could be yet another one of those Romans 8:28 situations, where God uses all things to work for good. Perhaps the many troubles of our country and world—including illness, civil unrest, and unemployment, just to name a few—will cause folks who haven't taken faith matters seriously to give more thought and prayer to the reality of good and evil, both God and the devil. That's why Fr. Lampert's book is not only so timely but so badly needed in a world that knows little about the source of gloom and doom or how to fight it. He brilliantly outlines how the answers can be found in Jesus, Scripture, and the teachings of the Church."

TERESA TOMEO
Syndicated Catholic Talk Show Host and
Bestselling Catholic Author

"Fr. Vincent Lampert has been in the trenches of deliverance for fourteen years and speaks from experience."

FR. GARY THOMAS
Exorcist for the Diocese of San Jose, California

"Most who write about exorcism are fascinated by demons. Fr. Vincent Lampert is fascinated by Christ. His focus on the Lord of Love who goes in search of every lost sheep gives proper context to his dramatic stories of exorcism. It is a context of gratitude and hope rather than fear and obsession."

CY KELLETT
Host of Catholic Answers Live

"In this book, Fr. Lampert gives us a very balanced presentation of the Church's ministry of exorcism. It has the benefit of validation from his extensive experience, but to his great credit he never dogmatizes his own experience. On the contrary, he teaches from the Scripture as it is authentically interpreted by the Church's authority. He introduces us to the rites of the Church and her official teaching. Furthermore, Lampert neither presents this teaching abstractly, nor seeks to spice it up like a Hollywood drama, but offers a very useful pastoral application to help us deepen our own relationship with Jesus Christ. For those who are wondering about the Church's ministry of exorcism, this is the book to consult for the most balanced and dependable teaching."

FR. BONIFACE HICKS, OSB
Host of We Are One Body *and Co-Author of*
Personal Prayer: A Guide for Receiving the Father's Love

"In *Exorcism*, Fr. Vincent Lampert has provided an insightful primer by which to better grasp the machinations of the devil in real time, not only for priests in their sacerdotal ministry but also for anyone seriously journeying the course of faith. Thoughtfully drawing from Sacred Scripture, the tradition of the Church, and his own vast experience, Fr. Lampert speaks to the spiritual battles prevalent in our day while reassuring the reader of the great love God has for each of us. A useful resource for the spiritual journey."

VERY REVEREND JEFFREY GROB, JCD
Judicial Vicar, Archdiocese of Chicago

·❦·

Series Editor: Fr. David Vincent Meconi, S.J.

Fr. David Vincent Meconi, S.J., is a Jesuit priest and professor of theology at Saint Louis University where he also serves as the Director of the Catholic Studies Centre. He is the editor of *Homiletic and Pastoral Review* and has published widely in the areas of Church history and Catholic culture. He holds the pontifical license in Patristics from the University of Innsbruck in Austria, and the D.Phil. in Ecclesiastical History from the University of Oxford.

About the Series

The great Christian Tradition has always affirmed that the world in which we live is a reflection of its divine source, a place perhaps torn apart by sin but still charged with busy and bustling creatures disclosing the beautiful presence of God. The *Living Faith* series consists of eminent Catholic authors who seek to help Christians navigate their way in this world. How do we understand objective truth in a culture insistent on relativism? How does one evangelize in a world offended when invited to something higher? How do we understand sin and salvation when so many have no real interest in becoming saints? The *Living Faith* series will answer these and numerous other questions Christians have today as they set out not only to live holy lives themselves, but to bring others to the fullness of life in Christ Jesus.

EXORCISM

EXORCISM

➤✳⳥

THE BATTLE AGAINST
SATAN AND HIS DEMONS

Fr. Vincent Lampert

EMMAUS
ROAD
PUBLISHING

Steubenville, Ohio
www.emmausroad.org

Emmaus Road Publishing
1468 Parkview Circle
Steubenville, Ohio 43952

Library of Congress Control Number: 2020944023.
ISBN: 978-1-64585-061-8 (pbk) / 978-1-64585-062-5 (ebook)

Cover design and layout by Emily Demary
Cover image: *Archangel Overwhelming the Demon* by Antonio Vivarini,
(ca. 1432 – ca. 1499)

TABLE OF CONTENTS

INTRODUCTION

One of my favorite definitions of the Church is that it is the guardian to the tree of life. Ever since Adam and Eve were banished from paradise, the human person has been on a journey to arrive at the tree of life and be united with God for all eternity in heaven. In the Book of Genesis, the first book of the Bible, we read, "Therefore the Lord God sent him forth from the garden of Eden, to till the ground from which he was taken. He drove out the man; and at the east of the garden of Eden he placed the cherubim, and a flaming sword which turned every way, to guard the way to the tree of life" (3:23–24). In the Book of Revelation, the last book of the Bible, we are told, "Blessed are those who wash their robes, that they may have the right to the tree of life and that they may enter the city by the gates" (22:14). What these passages teach us is that all of us are on a journey, with the ultimate destination being the tree of life and union with God.

We are not alone on this journey because Christ has given us the Church. The Church exists for the good of the human person. It is the vehicle that allows us to stay connected with God and to be protected from the evil one as we make our journey to the tree of life. The Church is the Bride of Christ that tells us that our true dignity is found with God, and apart from God the human person becomes distorted. The devil does everything in his power to destroy the Church, because he knows that if the Church is eliminated then we will get lost and stray from the path that God has laid out for us. Through his ordinary and extraordinary activity, the devil wants to trip us up, to lose our way, believing that if we get spiritually lost we will not arrive at the tree of life and like him, and the other fallen angels, we will be damned for all eternity. A special weapon used by the Church in its battle against Satan and his angels is the ministry of exorcism.

The purpose in writing this book is to present the Catholic Church's perspective on the reality and influence of the devil and his angels and what should be the Christian response. It is my prayer that all those who read this book will deepen their own commitment to the Lord, especially those who may have distanced themselves from their Christian roots. Its purpose is not to focus on what the devil is trying to do to us, but rather to focus on the love that God has for each and every person created in his image and likeness. People are always fascinated by the devil. What is needed is a greater fascination with God!

In this ministry, I submit myself to God so he may use me to help people, who are up against the forces of evil, to experience the immense and unconditional love that God has for each and every person. Oftentimes people who are plagued by evil feel a certain unworthiness. Exorcism allows people to know the truth that anyone who wants to be found can never be lost to God.

I am grateful to so many people who have helped me over the years in the ministry of exorcism. An exorcist must feel the support of his bishop. I want to recognize the bishops of the Archdiocese of Indianapolis, Archbishop Daniel Buechlein, OSB, who first appointed me as an exorcist, Cardinal Joseph Tobin, and Archbishop Charles Thompson, who reappointed me to this ministry. I pay special tribute to Msgr. John Ryan, the former exorcist of Indianapolis, and the Sisters of St. Francis in Oldenburg, Indiana, who first planted in me the seeds of priesthood. One of my greatest assets is Mrs. Mary Chasteen. She works very closely with me in this ministry helping to respond to so many emails, phone calls, and letters. She is the first line of contact for those seeking help, and I am fond of referring to her as my 'exorcistant.' No exorcist works alone, and she is an invaluable colleague in this ministry.

The Call to Be an Exorcist

On Sunday mornings, in every major city and small town across America, a sound begins to echo throughout the air. It is the ringing of church bells, a sound meant to remind us that we are called to wake up with the Church and to be about the things of God. It is a sad reality that far too many people today seem to be spiritually asleep. Many who have been baptized have abandoned their faith and lost the sense of the sacred in their lives. A 2019 Pew Research Center survey reported that 51 percent of millennials no longer identify themselves as Christians, and four out of ten millennials no longer identify with any religion. Some of the respondents say they are spiritual but no longer need to go to church, while others now profess to be atheists.

At a time when people have lost touch with their Christian heritage, there is a great risk of falling for ideas that sound appealing but that are actually misleading and extremely dangerous. St. Paul warns that "Satan disguises himself as an angel of light" and deceives many people (2 Cor 11:14–15). We must realize that the presence of the devil is sharpened as humanity and society distance ourselves from God. Truthfully, one is either in a relationship with God or with something else.

As the gap grows between the human person and God there has been a resurgence in the practice of magic and things centering on the occult. These things are viewed as attractive while belief in God has become unattractive. The danger we face is that when a person no longer believes in God, they are at risk for believing anything and everything. The result of rejecting God and embracing the occult is that people are opening themselves up to the forces of evil. What all of us must realize is that our ultimate identity comes from a relationship with God and not apart from him. God must not be viewed as a threat to the human person but the one who helps us to understand what it truly means to be human. Faith in God will lead us in one direction and the lack of faith in another. I believe people today need a renewed fascination with God, to see his presence around us rather than focusing on the reality of evil. It is once again time for all of us to focus on the positive aspects of our Catholic faith. As John the Apostle said, "he who is in you is greater than he who is in the world" (1 John 4:4).

The truth today is that far too many people live with a distorted view of freedom that echoes the fall of humanity, as mentioned in the Book of Genesis. The guiding principles of this distorted view of freedom are: You may do all you wish, no one has the right to command you, and you are the god of yourself. This viewpoint leaves no room for the one true God, and the result is a greater presence of evil both in the world and in the lives of individuals. To put it another way, the triumph of the devil is individualism, whereby the human person eliminates God from the picture and no longer accepts any external principles. Truth becomes internal and something of our own making. A clear example of this is abortion. God's truth regarding the sanctity of all human life, especially the unborn, is ignored and all that matters is one's so-called reproductive freedom.

We all have freedom, but it must be used in a responsible manner. Freedom does not mean that we can do whatever we want to do. Freedom and obedience to God go hand in hand. When we live in the manner that God has created us to live, being obedient to his commands, that is freedom in the true sense of the word. A distorted view of freedom happens when we act independently of God, believing that we are in control and can create our own version of what is morally good. As a result, we end up becoming slaves to our own passions and desires. In the Garden of Eden, the serpent says to Eve:

> "Did God say, 'You shall not eat of any tree of the garden'?" And the woman said to the serpent, "We may eat of the fruit of the trees of the garden; but

God said, 'You shall not eat of the fruit of the tree
which is in the midst of the garden, neither shall you
touch it, lest you die.'" But the serpent said to the
woman, 'You will not die. For God knows that when
you eat of it your eyes will be opened, and you will be
like God . . .'" (Gen 3:2–5).

Falling to the lies of the devil and failing to obey the
commands of God, Adam and Eve lost the true sense of what
it meant to be free. This pattern of losing the true sense of
what it means to be free continues today; when we, like our
first parents, choose to believe the lies of the evil one and
sink into individualism.

I was appointed to be the exorcist for the Archdiocese
of Indianapolis back in 2005. At the time, I became one of
about a dozen officially appointed exorcists in the United
States. Today that number has grown to around 125. The ex-
act number is unknown as some exorcists are named publicly
whereas others choose to remain anonymous. The appointment of an exorcist for a particular diocese is important because it tells people the Church is listening and is concerned
for their spiritual welfare.

Prior to 1972, every man preparing for the priesthood
received the minor order of exorcist. It was viewed as one
of the steps toward ordination. In 1972, Pope St. Paul VI
eliminated the minor order of exorcist in his Apostolic Letter
Ministeria Quaedam. Of note in this document is that the

pope, while eliminating the minor order of exorcist as an office universal in the Latin Church, states that the conference of bishops for a particular region could request of the Apostolic See to establish exorcist as a ministry in their area if they deemed it necessary or useful.[1]

People often ask me how I ended up being the exorcist for my diocese. I jokingly respond that I was in the wrong place at the wrong time. In July of 2005, Msgr. John Ryan, the exorcist for Indianapolis, passed away. He was a very holy and devout priest. I knew him as a child as he was the pastor of St. Anthony Parish in Indianapolis where I attended eighth grade. Many of the priests knew that Archbishop Daniel Buechlein, the Archbishop of Indianapolis, was looking to name his replacement, and I think we were all trying to stay under the radar. I was attending a meeting at the archbishop's residence when he looked at me and said he was appointing me to be the exorcist for the archdiocese. I was a bit taken aback and even looked behind me to see if he was speaking to someone else. He knew I was planning to be on sabbatical in Rome in the early part of 2006 and said he wanted me to study and train on exorcism while I was there.

Archbishop Buechlein was a humble man who said he didn't know exactly what he was appointing me to, but since Indianapolis had always had an appointed exorcist he wanted

---

[1]   Pope Paul VI, Apostolic Letter given Motu Propio, *Ministeria Quaedam*, (August 15, 1972), § 5, available from http://www.vatican.va.

to keep the tradition. When I asked why he chose me, he indicated it was because he wanted a priest who believed in the reality of evil, but not one who would be too quick to believe that everyone who came to me was actually up against the forces of evil. Over the years, the archbishop and I had many good conversations about exorcism. When I would tell him that one of the younger priests wanted to be the exorcist he would smile and say, "I worry about anyone who would actually want the appointment." He told me the fact that I was not seeking to be the exorcist made me the best candidate. Archbishop Buechlein died in 2018 after a battle with cancer. In my final meeting with him, true to his humility, he smiled and said he was sorry for what he had gotten me into. We both had a good laugh.

When I arrived in Rome in February of 2006, I was blessed to become acquainted with Fr. Gary Thomas from San Jose, California. Recently, he also had been appointed the exorcist of his diocese. He proved to be a great resource in helping me to locate an exorcist in Rome who was willing to allow me to do an apprenticeship under him. Fr. Thomas has become a good friend and is a tremendous colleague in this ministry. He has done much to promote the need for more exorcists to be appointed throughout the United States.

Over the three month period I was in Rome, the Franciscan priest who mentored me allowed me to observe forty exorcisms and to learn firsthand the Church's ministry to those who were facing the forces of evil and were seeking the help of the Church. I will be forever grateful for his kindness and his willingness to take me under his charge. Since that initial training, I have furthered my education by attending the Vatican course on exorcism and have become a member of the International Association of Exorcists. This group of priests and their auxiliaries from throughout the world gathers every other year in Rome for the opportunity to foster collegiality and for on-going training and formation.

In my early days of this ministry, I would receive about 100 inquiries annually from people who believed they were dealing with the demonic. Currently, I receive more than 1800 calls, emails, and letters a year from people all over the country and even other parts of the world who are seeking help from the Church. These are Catholics and people who belong to other Christian faith traditions, world religions, or no religion whatsoever. The thing these people all share is that they are hurting and are seeking help from the Church.

Due to the volume of people who reach out to me, I am assisted in this ministry by Mrs. Mary Chasteen. Balancing exorcism ministry and the responsibilities of parish life can be a bit daunting at times. She acts as the first line of contact for those seeking help, and with her theological background in the area of exorcism, often she is able to answer the questions people have or to direct them to an exorcist in their geographic area without me ever having to get involved. She exemplifies the following qualities that an exorcist seeks in those who assist him in this ministry:

- Be a practicing Catholic
- Have a life rooted in prayer and the reading of Sacred Scripture
- Possess a strong moral character
- Have a strong desire to spread the Good News of Jesus Christ
- Be well known by the exorcist
- Know well their role as a collaborator in this ministry
- Have a strong knowledge of the faith and be able to articulate it to others
- Be constantly growing in the knowledge and understanding of the practice of exorcism
- Is discreet, humble, patient, and kind
- Does not try to take the role of the exorcist
- Maintain confidentiality

Even though people may want to talk directly with me, they need to understand that I do not have any special powers or abilities. The power to confront demons and to cast them out rests in the name of Jesus Christ and the authority he has given to the Church. Indeed, in an exorcism Jesus is not a bystander—he is the Main Actor. Before I departed from Rome to head back to the States, the priest who trained me left me with these final words, "When you're doing an exorcism and even think for a split moment, 'wow, look at what I'm doing,' you've just walked on unholy ground. The focus must never be on the exorcist. The focus is always on Jesus Christ and his power and authority." This is sound advice that I have always taken to heart. In this ministry it would be so easy to inflate one's ego when it comes to combatting Satan and his angels. Humility coupled with a servant's heart must be the key ingredients in the life of an exorcist.

WHO IS THE DEVIL?

B elief in the existence and activity of angels and demons
is a common religious fact within many cultural traditions. At the same time, there are many people who reject the
notion of angelic creatures and believe the existence of angels
and demons, along with exorcism and demonic possession,
comes out of a primitive, superstitious worldview, as a relic
from the time of Christ, a throwback to the Middle Ages,
or to a time when mental health issues were not well under-
stood. For some people today, including those in the Church,
to even talk about the existence of the devil is an embarrass-
ment. For these people, evil is something of our own making.
They believe it is nothing more than humanity's inhumane
treatment of one another. There are also those who look at
things from a purely scientific viewpoint that says, "seeing is
believing." Yet for people of faith, we look at things from the
viewpoint that says, "believing is seeing." The basis of what
we believe comes to us from Sacred Scripture and throughout the Bible there are many accounts of the devil's attempts

to thwart the coming of the Kingdom of God. Therefore, by asserting the existence of the devil, the Church is remaining faithful to the Bible.

After the Second Vatican Council (1962–1965), the existence of angels and demons was really called into question. With the secularization of society, the general thought was that if one did not accept some spiritual aspect, then it was not true or relevant. Interestingly, the Second Vatican Council references the devil more than any other council. There are references to the devil in the great documents of *Lumen gentium*, *Gaudium et spes*, *Ad gentes*, and *Sacrosanctum concilium*. Indeed, in the Catholic tradition, Sacred Scripture and the Magisterium of the Church consistently confirm the truth of the existence of angels and demons. The Catechism of the Catholic Church states "that God 'from the beginning of time made at once (*simul*) out of nothing both orders of creatures, the spiritual and the corporeal, that is, the angelic and the earthly' [Lateran Council IV (1215): DS 800; cf. DS 3002 and Paul VI, *CPG* § 8]" (327). The mystery of the human person is linked to these angelic creatures. They are a transcendent reality that lets us humans know that we are not alone in the universe. Our belief in angels and demons helps us to grow in our knowledge of God, his majesty and power, and the immensity of the love that he has for the human person created in his image and likeness.

Scripture provides much evidence for the existence of

demons. A major theme throughout the New Testament is a clash between the Kingdom of God and the kingdom of Satan. Jesus is a name that means "God saves." The traditional title of Jesus as Savior or Redeemer reminds us that Jesus saves and rescues us from a real danger, from something evil. One of the major reasons Jesus became human was to free us from demonic influence. Indeed, his ministry is one of exorcism. We read in the First Letter of John, "The reason the Son of God appeared was to destroy the works of the devil" (3:8). St. Paul in writing to the Ephesians says, "For we are not contending against flesh and blood, but against the principalities, against the powers, against the world rulers of this present darkness, against the spiritual hosts of wickedness in the heavenly places" (6:12). In the Acts of the Apostles we read, "how God anointed Jesus of Nazareth with the Holy Spirit and with power how he went about doing good and healing all that were oppressed by the devil, for God was with him" (10:38). These passages clearly illustrate the fact that the world that Jesus encountered was saturated with demons, and he came to exorcize them. Jesus shared this power of exorcism with his disciples for when he sent them out he "gave them authority over unclean spirits, to cast them out, and to heal every disease and every infirmity" (Matt 10:1).

There are those who say that Jesus knew the people he encountered were not truly possessed and that he was only going along with the sentiment of the day that demons were real.

This reads too much into the sacred text. If Jesus makes the distinction between evil spirits and sickness, then we should make the distinction as well and recognize the reality of these spiritual creatures. In truth, confrontation with the devil is a common theme throughout Jesus' life. If we do not accept the reality of the devil, why would we accept anything of the Gospel? Jesus did not tell us that the devil was a metaphor for evil or a superstition. Through his ministry he tells us that the devil is real. Indeed, the work of Jesus is incomprehensible without the reality of the devil. To state it bluntly, the devil is real, and his existence is a matter of faith.

When it comes to the existence of demons, Pope St. Paul VI, back in 1972, stated clearly that "evil is not merely an absence of something but an active force, a living, spiritual being that is perverted and perverts others." He went on to say,

> "It is a departure from the teaching of the Bible and the Church to refuse to acknowledge the Devil's existence . . . or to explain the Devil as a pseudo-reality, a conceptual, fanciful personification of the unknown causes of our misfortunes. . . . Many passages in the Gospel show us that we are dealing not just with one Devil, but with many (Luke 11:21; Mark 5:9). But the principal one is Satan, which means the adversary, the enemy; and along with him are many others, all of them creatures of God, but fallen because they rebelled and were damned; a whole mysterious world,

convulsed by a most unfortunate drama about which we know very little."[1]

These thoughts are reflected in the Catechism of the Catholic Church where it states that "evil is not an abstraction, but refers to a person, Satan, the Evil One, the angel who opposes God" (2851).

Pope St. John Paul II also elaborated on the reality of the devil in his General Audience on August 13, 1986 stating that the annunciation of the Gospel is the defeat of Satan. He went on to say that the presence of the devil is sharpened as humanity and society are distancing ourselves from God. Although this can be somewhat alarming, the Holy Father provides us with a sense of hope when he goes on to remind us that the power of Satan is not infinite, it is limited due to the fact he is only a creature. Certainly powerful as a spirit, but still a creature whose power cannot annul the power of God.

Building on the teachings of his predecessors, Pope Francis, in his Apostolic Exhortation on the Call to Holiness in the Contemporary World, *Gaudete et Exsultate*, says that "we should not think of the devil as a myth, a representation, a symbol, a figure of speech or an idea" (GE n. 161). In his homily at Mass on Friday, April 11, 2014, Pope Francis stated, "the devil also exists in the 21st century, and we need to

---

[1] Pope Paul VI, General Audience (November 15, 1972). https://www.papalencyclicals.net/paul06/p6devil.htm

learn from the Gospel how to battle against him." He further stated that "We must not be 'naive' about his ways. In fact, we need to be very aware of the strategies he employs to entrap us. For the devil is not a thing of the past." The devil's cleverest ruse, according to the famous remark by the nineteenth-century French poet, Charles Pierre Baudelaire, as echoed by St. John Paul II and Pope Francis, is to convince us that he does not exist.

The Preamble of the Rite of Exorcism, *Exorcisms and Related Supplications,* states, "Throughout the entire course of the history of salvation, angelic creatures have been present, some serving the divine plan and continually bringing the Church hidden and powerful assistance, but others, the fallen ones, also called *diabolical,* who are opposed to God and his salvific will and his work accomplished in Christ, trying to associate human beings in their revolt against God." These words are derived from the Catechism of the Catholic Church where the existence of angelic creatures constitutes part of the Creed that is recited at Sunday Mass, "I believe in one God, the Father Almighty, maker of heaven and earth, of all things visible and invisible."

These invisible creatures have fascinated the human mind down through the ages and we have always sought to better understand the angelic order. St. Cyril of Jerusalem (c. AD 313–386) first mentions the nine angelic orders to the newly baptized in his *Mystagogic Catecheses.* Pseudo-Dionysius the

Areopagite (AD 5th–6th century) in his *Celestial Hierarchy*, gave a more detailed description of the angelic order, identifying its authority structures, powers, and domains. His work strongly influenced St. Thomas Aquinas (AD 1225–1274) and would popularize the idea of three hierarchies composed of nine choirs. The first hierarchy consists of the choirs of Seraphim, Cherubim, and Thrones. The second hierarchy consists of the choirs of Dominations, Virtues, and Powers. The third hierarchy is comprised of the choirs of Principalities, Archangels, and Angels.[2]

There is no biblical account of the creation of the angels. Much of our understanding of the angelic order comes to us from one of the great saints of the Church, St. Augustine. His works, *The Literal Meaning of Genesis* (AD 404–412) and *The City of God* (AD 413–427), provide us with an interesting reflection on the creation of angels. In the Book of Genesis we read, "And God said, 'Let there be light'; and there was light. And God saw that the light was good; and God separated the light from the darkness. God called the light Day, and the darkness he called Night" (1:3–5). From this passage, St. Augustine believed that the light first created by God that was found to be good was the angelic order. When the light was separated into day and night St. Augustine saw this as the judgment of the angelic order because the

---

[2] Serge-Thomas Bonino, OP. *Angels and Demons: A Catholic Introduction* (Washington, DC: The Catholic University of America Press, 2016), 254.

separation was not stated to be good. God's angelic order had now been separated into angels and demons.[3]

Angels are purely intellectual creatures that received infused knowledge from the moment they were created. Put another way, from the first moment of their creation the angels were in the presence of all they can know. For them there is no process of learning. Much like a computer receives information by download, angels received knowledge directly from God. With this knowledge they could use their free will to either accept or to reject God. They could go their own way or choose to follow the path that God had laid out for them that would lead to glory.

St. Thomas Aquinas distinguishes between Evening Knowledge and Morning Knowledge.[4] Evening Knowledge refers to what angels can know in the natural order. This knowledge is considered imperfect because it can be used to act independent of God. Morning Knowledge refers to what the angels can know in the supernatural order. This knowledge is considered perfect because it demonstrates that one has freely chosen to act dependent on God. Evening Knowledge was present to the angels from the outset of their creation, but Morning Knowledge was not. Only when angels used their Evening Knowledge to turn to God did they receive

---

[3] Bonino, *Angels and Demons*, 53.

[4] Thomas Aquinas, *Basic Writings of Saint Thomas Aquinas*, Volume One, ed. Anton C. Pegis (Indianapolis/Cambridge: Hackett Publishing Company, 1997), q. 58.

Morning Knowledge and thus complete their creation by becoming blessed. Think of the story of creation in the Book of Genesis. Only when evening came and morning followed was it a new day. The angels who chose to use their Evening Knowledge to turn from God did not complete their creation according to God's plan. Deprived of Morning Knowledge of their own free choice, their minds were darkened, and they became the fallen angels.

The first of the fallen angels, Lucifer, was before the fall the most exalted of all the angels. After the fall he became the chief of the evil spirits now referred to as the devil or Satan. The word *devil* comes from the Greek word *diabolos* which means adversary, slanderer, opposer. The word *Satan* comes from Hebrew and means accuser. Satan is a morally wicked creature, hostile to both humans and God. He is not wicked by nature, but because of vice, as the Book of Wisdom declares, "through the devil's envy death entered the world, and those who belong to his party experience it" (2:24).[5]

The devil is an illusionist who demonstrates false reality. He makes people see things that amaze and fascinate in order to win the person over. Matthew's Gospel brands him as "the Evil One" (5:37). In John's Gospel, Jesus prays asking the Father to keep his disciples "from the evil one" (17:15). Matthew also refers to him as "the enemy" who sowed the

5   Bonino, *Angels and Demons*, 27.

weeds into the field (13:39). John's Gospel says that the devil "was a murderer from the beginning, and has nothing to do with the truth, because there is no truth in him. When he lies, he speaks according to his own nature, for he is a liar and the father of lies" (John 8:44). The Book of Revelation refers to the devil as "a great red dragon, with seven heads and ten horns, and seven diadems upon his heads" (12:3). It also says of him that he is "the deceiver of the whole world" (12:9) and "the dragon, that ancient serpent, who is the Devil and Satan" (Rev 20:2).

Lucifer was the most brilliant and most beautiful of all created beings in heaven. The Book of the Prophet Ezekiel compares the pride of the King of Tyre to the pride of Satan after the fall:

> You were the signet of perfection, full of wisdom and perfect in beauty. You were in Eden, the garden of God; every precious stone was your covering, carnelian, topaz, and jasper, chrysolite, beryl, and onyx, sapphire, carbuncle, and emerald; and wrought in gold were your settings and your engravings. On the day that you were created they were prepared. With an anointed guardian cherub I placed you; you were on the holy mountain of God; in the midst of the stones of fire you walked. You were blameless in your ways from the day you were created, till iniquity was found in you. In the abundance of your trade you

were filled with violence, and you sinned; so I cast you as a profane thing from the mountain of God, and the guardian cherub drove you out from the midst of the stones of fire. Your heart was proud because of your beauty; you corrupted your wisdom for the sake of your splendor. I cast you to the ground. (28:12–17)

Lucifer, like all angels, was created for the purpose of glorifying God. However, instead of serving God and praising him forever, he desired to rule over heaven and all creation in the place of God. He wanted supreme authority. The Fathers of the Church see in the Book of the Prophet Isaiah a reference to Lucifer where it says, "How you are fallen from heaven, O Day Star, son of Dawn! How you are cut down to the ground, you who laid the nations low! You said in your heart, 'I will ascend to heaven: above the stars of God I will set my throne on high; I will sit on the mount of assembly in the far north; I will ascend above the heights of the clouds, I will make myself like the Most High.' But you are brought down to Sheol, to the depths of the Pit" (14:12–15). The key word in this passage is "I" which is why we say the sin of Lucifer was the sin of pride.

Lucifer did not care what God desired for him. He wanted to act independent from his Creator. All that mattered to him was what he desired for himself and what he wanted the most was to resemble God and become an end unto himself.

Therefore, in the words of John of St. Thomas, Lucifer used his free will, choosing to remain the first in an inferior order rather than to become one among others in a superior order.[6] During my training in Rome, I once asked my mentor what was the most difficult case of possession that he had dealt with. He shared with me that once during an exorcism he asked the demon its name. Getting no response, he asked if the demon's name was Lucifer. The demon responded that he had once been known by that name but no longer. In rejecting God, Lucifer was no longer known by this name for to recognize the name "Lucifer" is to recognize the One who gave the name. Lucifer had rejected God and became the devil, or Satan.

Satan's sin involves the sin of many angels. Since angels are depicted as light (based on the writings of St. Augustine and his understanding of the Genesis account of creation) they are sometimes referred to as stars. The Book of Revelation declares that the great red dragon's tail "swept down a third of the stars of heaven, and cast them to the earth" (12:4). How was it that Satan influenced one third of the angelic choir to join him in his rebellion against God? The answer is that angels in a higher choir illumine those in a lower choir. Since Lucifer was closest to the Throne of God when he rebelled against God, his choice reverberated throughout the entire angelic choir. The choice he had made was now

---

[6] Bonino, *Angels and Demons*, 206.

presented in their own minds. Using their own free will they chose to make it their own. The result was that by following the example of Lucifer to rebel against God they now surrendered themselves to Satan as their chief and became his angels.

It is important to state that demons are not evil by nature, since as angelic creatures they owe their origin to God. Everything that God created is good in its nature. The Fourth Lateran Council (AD 1215) makes it clear that the evil found in demons is due to their own free choice and not something that came from God. The Letter of Jude states that the demons are "the angels that did not keep to their own position but left their proper dwelling" (1:6). They are called evil because they used their free will in such a way as to reject God, thus distorting their original goodness as intended by God. In other words, the evil found in demons comes from their opposition to allowing their intellects to be shaped by God and his love. Angels are filled with intellectual knowledge and love. Demons are filled with intellectual knowledge and hate.

After the fall, the demons do not lose their angelic intellect (Evening Knowledge) but their minds now become darkened. In rejecting God, the source of virtue and enlightenment, they are deprived of the light of wisdom and fall into darkness. I want to point out that an angel from a lower choir is stronger than a fallen angel from a higher choir. The reason is that an angel possesses both Evening and Morning Knowledge, whereas a fallen angel possesses only Evening Knowledge. Thus, angels are perfect creatures and fallen angels are not. Therefore, it can be said that one's Guardian Angel is more powerful than the devil himself. This is also the basis for the belief that St. Michael, who belonged to the eighth choir of Archangels, was able to challenge Satan, who fell from the first choir of the Seraphim. Another contrast to the fallen angels who fell into darkness are the saints of the Church who are depicted in light. The halos that surround their heads are a sign that they have allowed themselves to be enlightened by the glory of God. The light they transmit does not come from themselves. Its source is God himself. By choosing to embrace the wisdom of God and living it out they are confirmed in salvation whereas Satan and his angels, who chose to reject the wisdom of God, are confirmed in damnation.

It is often asked if the demons could ever repent of their sin. The answer is no. The free will of the demons to sin against God persists forever. They are incapable of repenting, there is no redemption, and their damnation is eternal. This is the case because unlike humans, whose free will can change by growing in knowledge and virtue, demons, due to their purely intellectual nature, are situated from the start in the presence of all that they can know.[7] As stated earlier,

---

[7] Bonino, *Angels and Demons*, 212.

there is no process of learning. Once they make a choice utilizing their free will, they remain fixed on that choice forever. It would never even occur to a demon to seek forgiveness. The Catechism of the Catholic Church says: "'There is no repentance for the angels after their fall, just as there is no repentance for men after death' [St. John Damascene, *De Fide orth.* 2, 4: PG 94, 877]" (393).

After their expulsion from heaven, the evil spirits focus their attention on humans and battle with the Church. There is no sense of fraternity in the demonic world. They hate each other but are united in their hatred for God and humans. Therefore, it is common for them to work in groups under the direction of a demon of a higher hierarchical rank. They realize that we have the potential for that which they have rejected; namely, to be with God for all eternity. Their desire is that we would make the same choice that they themselves have made and reject God. It is the old adage that "misery loves company." Their activity of getting us to join in their misery is classified as either extraordinary or ordinary.

THE EXTRAORDINARY
ACTIVITY OF THE DEVIL

The devil is a conscious force who knows, wills, and pursues a destructive goal.[1] He does everything to oppose the coming of the Kingdom of God. If God is for something; the devil is against it. Fr. Gabriele Amorth says that the main goal of the devil is "to distance us from God, from the sacraments, and from everything that is good."[2] He does this by using specialized attacks against us that fall under the categories of infestation, vexation, obsession, and possession.

Demonic infestation is the presence of evil in a location, object, or animal. It is caused when something of an evil nature has occurred in a particular place or when one has brought some item associated with the occult into the home.

---

[1] Cardinal Léon-Joseph Suenens, *Renewal and the Powers of Darkness* [Malines Document IV] (London: Darton, Longman and Todd, 1983), 7.

[2] Gabriele Amorth, *Father Amorth: My Battle Against Satan*, with Elisabetta Fezzi, trans. Charlotte J. Fasi (Manchester, NH: Sophia Institute Press, 2017), 45.

When evil is manifesting in a location, there are unexplained noises, such as footsteps, voices, laughter, and doors and windows opening and closing. It can also include things like insect invasions, lights and other electronic devices turning on and off for no apparent reason, objects disappearing from one location and reappearing in another, pictures falling off the walls, furniture moving, seeing dark shadowy figures, and objects, like chairs and blankets, levitating in the air.

I want to say something about restless spirits. A clear distinction needs to be made between them and evil spirits. An evil spirit is a fallen angel, whereas a restless spirit is the soul of one who has died. People often ask if it is possible for the spirit of a departed loved one to still interact with us by manifesting in a location. Let's be clear that when we die we cannot choose of our own accord to continue being present in this world. God alone can permit that, and his reasons are known to him alone. Exorcists will tell you that 99.9 percent of the time when people talk about infestation it pertains to evil spirits. However, a small percentage can be attributed to loved ones who God is permitting to reach out to us for prayer and nothing more. When it is a demon infesting a location, people have a sense of fear. When it is a restless spirit, fear is not present.

Once a woman told me that her house was haunted because items were being moved in her home and she would hear footsteps and knocking. It was more annoying than fearful. She shared with me that her former husband had died shortly after going through a nasty divorce. A few months after he moved out, he was diagnosed with terminal cancer. Before his death he sought reconciliation with her by apologizing for how he had treated her. Her final words to him before he moved out were that he could burn in hell. It was after his death that the noises began. She was angry about how he had treated her. Once she let go of the hurt and told him that she forgave him all the noises in the house ceased. It is my experience that once a restless spirit receives the prayers that it needs, closure comes about, and it no longer manifests.

On another occasion, I worked with several families in a neighborhood who saw spirits in their homes of a family who had been murdered 100 years previously. They could tell me their names and describe their features. Doing some research, it was discovered that the new subdivision was built on farmland where a family had been killed by an intruder. Offering prayers for the family that they would rest in peace caused the restless spirits to depart.

Infestation connected with an object has to do with items that may have been cursed or those that are used in occult practices, such as a voodoo doll. The basis for the belief that animals can be infested is based on the story of the Gerasene Demoniac in Mark's Gospel when Jesus sends the unclean spirits into the herd of swine (5:13). When it comes to demonic infestation the best course of action is to have the house or building and its contents blessed using some type of specialized deliverance prayer.[3] If it is an animal or an object, I would offer a prayer as well asking God to break the connection with the demonic. In cases where the object is associated with magic it should always be destroyed. A prayer is said over the object, it is blessed with holy water and then burned.

Demonic vexations are physical attacks that a person experiences. One who is being attacked physically by a demon will exhibit on the body cuts, burns, scrapes, bruises, swellings, and in some cases incisions of letters that appear on the skin that persist for some time and then disappear. Vexation can also affect a person's health, causing sickness without any apparent cause. The cause of this particular type of extraordinary activity on the part of the devil is due to a curse or a person's lack of virtue and commitment to God. People open themselves to these attacks by being weak in their faith to such a degree that the actions used against them to cause harm, relying on the power of magic, are effective. It is also

[3] When blessing a location, I have the family gather by the main door and then offer the following or similar prayer: "Good and gracious God I ask you to drive away and cast out from under this roof the presence of any and all evil spirits. Command them to depart and to never return again. Protect and safeguard this family who call upon your Holy Name. By your Cross you have conquered Satan and his angels. May this family always delight in your Divine help. Amen." I will then bless the family and go to each room of the house and bless it with holy water saying, "God, I ask your blessing upon this room. Fill it with your presence and banish from it any presence of evil. In the name of the Father, and of the Son, and of the Holy Spirit. Amen."

possible that the opening is created through behavior that goes against God's commands, such as frequenting psychics, mediums, fortunetellers, brujas, curanderos, and dabbling in magic that includes spells and curses. Sometimes vexations can strike at one's affections, causing a married or engaged couple to breakup. They can also impact one's work and friendships.[4] In these situations, exorcism prayers should be offered and the afflicted person must express a desire to grow in faith and virtue or renounce whatever they may have done to cause the attacks, such as visiting the psychic.

In cases pertaining to relationships and employment, the priest should break the curse or spell by declaring in his prayer over the person, "As a priest of Jesus Christ, I hereby declare null and void any curses, spells, or hexes that may have been placed upon you." Priesthood carries with it sacramental power, and a priest should never be hesitant to utilize the sacred character bestowed on him through the Sacrament of Holy Orders. Truthfully, if a priest takes his priesthood seriously, so will the devil. The converse is also true, if a priest does not take his priesthood seriously, neither will the devil.

I prefer to use the term *demonic vexation* as opposed to *demonic oppression* because vexation is something that one may bring upon themselves or that which is imposed by someone else. Oppression, on the other hand, is a gift from

---

4   Gabriele Amorth, *An Exorcist Explains the Demonic*, trans. Charlotte J. Fasi (Manchester, NH: Sophia Institute Press, 2016), 70.

God. It may sound strange to say that one experiencing demonic attacks is receiving a gift from God. Yet, there are examples, in Sacred Scripture and in the lives of the saints, of
people who did nothing wrong or who had no evil placed
upon them but who experienced attacks by the devil. God
permitted these holy men and women to undergo siege by the
devil as a form of spiritual purification. By suffering bodily
attacks through the actions of demons they grew in virtue
and saw the areas of their lives that still needed to be turned
over to God. These people were not viewed as possessed and
certainly did not need exorcism. The demonic torment they
were undergoing was leading them to sanctification.

We can think of Job in the Old Testament whom God
permitted to be afflicted by the devil as a way to show his
fidelity to God. When Job had lost everything, those around
him told him to "curse God, and die" (Job 2:9). He responds
by saying, "Shall we receive good at the hand of God, and shall
we not receive evil" (Job 2:10). In other words, his response to
his oppression was "if things be good I glorify God; if things
be bad I glorify God." His personal circumstances had no
bearing on God's rightful place in his life. Because he was a
virtuous man who endured his demonic suffering, we are told
that, "the Lord restored the fortunes of Job" (Job 42:10).

The Apostle Paul also experienced demonic oppression
as he worked to spread the Gospel. In his Second Letter to
the Corinthians he writes, "And to keep me from being too

elated by the abundance of revelations, a thorn was given me in the flesh, a messenger of Satan, to harass me, to keep me from being too elated" (12:7). Countless other saints also experienced demonic oppression throughout their lives.

One of the best examples is St. Pio of Pietrelcina, affectionately known as Padre Pio. From an early age he felt the call to religious life and experienced an exhausting interior struggle. On one occasion, he has a vision where he sees a man that he is told he must do battle against. Turning to prayer, God says to him, "All resistance is useless, it is advisable that you fight this man. Take heart; enter confidently into the combat, go forward courageously, for I shall be close to you. I will assist you and not allow him to overcome you."[5] St. Pio knows the man that he must do battle with is Satan. Throughout his life he experiences many demonic attacks from the devil who he refers to as 'Bluebeard.' St. Pio writes, "I cannot tell you how many times he has thrown me out of bed, and dragged me around the room."[6] The pain and suffering that St. Pio went through was not because he had done something wrong to create a connection with evil. On the contrary, God permitted it to allow him to grow in holiness and virtue. Remaining steadfast to God amid his struggles, he would become a shining light bringing countless souls to Christ.

5   Tarcisio Cervinara, *The Devil in the Life of Padre Pio* (San Giovanni Rotondo: Edizioni Padre Pio da Pietrelcina, 2009), 59.

6   Cervinara, *The Devil in the Life of Padre Pio*, 74.

What is said of St. Pio is true of all the holy men and women through the ages who experienced demonic oppression. Their strength and fortitude in the face of the devil's attacks helped others to enter into a relationship with Jesus Christ. St. Justin Martyr (AD 100–165) touches on this subject where he writes, "These spirits whom we call demons strive for nothing else than to alienate men from God their Creator, and from Christ, His first-begotten. Indeed, they have clamped down those who are powerless to lift themselves above earthly conditions, and they still clamp them down to earthly things, and to manufactured idols. Besides, they even try to trip those who rise to the contemplation of divine things, and unless such persons are wise in their judgments and pure and passionless in their life, the demons will force them into ungodliness."[7]

Demonic obsessions are mental attacks that the devil uses to influence a person's external and internal senses. By impacting our imaginations, he can cause a person to see visions that are intended to cause fear, to entice one to commit sin, and to distract from the practice of virtue. A person experiencing obsession can have nightmares, hallucinations, obscene and blasphemous thoughts, and be fixated on things that pertain to the demonic, such as the number 666 or be convinced they have blasphemed against the Holy Spirit,

---

[7] St. Justin Martyr, *The First and Second Apologies*, trans. Leslie William Barnard (Mahwah, NJ: Paulist Press, 1997), 58.

which Jesus says is the only unforgiveable sin (Matt 12:31–32; Mark 3:28–29; Luke 12:10). People suffering from obsession can feel as if they are going insane. Oftentimes they become more and more depressed, sad, desperate, suicidal, mentally exhausted, and may have inclinations to harm others. Because obsession deals with one's mental capacities and how one sees oneself in relationship to the world, in the ministry of exorcism it is the most difficult extraordinary activity of the devil to assess. Therefore, people afflicted with obsession need a tandem approach and should see both a mental health professional as well as a priest for pastoral care.

The fourth and final type of extraordinary activity of the devil is demonic possession. It is the action whereby the devil or some other evil spirit takes control of a person's body, treating that body as if it were its own. Exorcists are trained to understand that once a demon reveals itself, the actions of the person are now wholly defined by the demon. There must be a clear distinction made between the actions of the person and those of the demon. For example, once a demon manifests through a person's body, I would never say that the afflicted person cursed me. It is the evil spirit who is doing that. When one is possessed, the evil spirit will move a person's tongue in order to speak, their feet in order to walk, their hands in order to write, attack, or offer obscene gestures. Those who suffer from demonic possession may lose all or part of their consciousness as to what is taking place. Some of the people

I have ministered to have told me that once the demon takes over their body, they are no longer aware of what is happening. Others have told me that they are aware of what is taking place but are powerless to stop it as they have become like prisoners, trapped in their own bodies.

The tradition of the Church has maintained four criteria in evaluating the validity of cases of demonic possession. The criteria are (1) the ability to speak and understand languages otherwise unknown to the individual, (2) exhibiting superhuman strength beyond the normal capacity of the individual, (3) having elevated perception with knowledge otherwise unknown to the individual, and (4) a strong resistance to anything of a sacred nature. These include such things as being shown a Bible, being in a sacred place, being shown a crucifix, or being blessed with holy water or a relic.

It is also possible to know that an evil spirit is present when symptoms of the demonic are observed. These include:

+ Bodily contortions, whereby the demon is revealing itself, such as the arching of the back
+ A change in the person's voice as it becomes much deeper and louder in order to instill fear
+ A change in physical appearance, such as foaming at the mouth and the eyes rolled in the back of the head, whereby the demon is demonstrating his power
+ Extremely foul odors as the demon reveals its wretched

and vile character

- A change in the temperature of the room whereby it becomes much colder, demonstrating their distance from God
- Uncontrollable laughter or screaming, also done to cause fear
- Hissing and the resemblance of the movement of a snake, demonstrating they are fallen creatures
- In some extreme cases, levitation, whereby the demon is trying to amaze his audience.

I still recall the first exorcism that I was able to witness. Sitting in a small room at a church in Rome, with the afflicted person and their spouse, the priest training me came in and placed a roll of paper towels on a table and tied a plastic grocery bag to a wall radiator. He made the Sign of the Cross and blessed the person. Immediately their eyes rolled in the back of their head, they began foaming at the mouth, and uttered blasphemies against God and the exorcist. Without even a slight trace of fear, the exorcist grabbed a paper towel, wiped off the person's mouth, and placed the towel in the plastic grocery bag. As the demon laughed hysterically and began to levitate, the priest put his hand on the person's head and pushed the manifesting demon back into the chair, all while never pausing with the exorcism prayers of the Church. I must say at that moment I thought, "What has my bishop gotten me into?"

All these manifestations can be indications of demonic possession, but it is important to understand that the exorcist is trained to be a skeptic. I should be the last one to believe that someone is possessed. Exorcists must arrive at moral certitude, meaning they must exhaust every other possible explanation for what is taking place in the life of the person and come to the point where they believe, beyond any reasonable doubt, that the person in front of them is truly possessed. This is extremely important because the Church could cause greater harm if she labels a person as being possessed and that label prevents the person from getting the true help they need either from their medical doctor or a mental health expert. Genuine cases of demonic possession are rare—they are real—they do happen—but not very frequently. Perhaps only one out of every five thousand cases is a true demonic possession. Most cases that I have dealt with are related to infestation, vexation, and obsession.

It amazes me what people believe demons are capable of when it comes to demonic possession. Their so-called powers and abilities need to be debunked. For example, we need to realize that possession is not contagious. Many people often ask me if I have ever feared during an exorcism that a demon will leave the afflicted person and go into me. Please realize that a demon cannot jump out of one person's body and go freely into another. That makes for a good movie, but it gives more credit to the demon than it deserves. Demonic possession comes about when people open themselves up to the forces of evil, and this can be done either directly or indirectly. This is done directly when one actively engages in activities that cultivate a relationship with evil spirits; and indirectly when one engages in activities that are meant just to be fun or entertaining, but in reality create a connection with evil spirits.

Any priest should be able to address cases of demonic infestation, vexation, and obsession by praying in the location or praying with and for the person troubled physically or mentally by evil. Cases that deal with demonic possession should be referred to the local bishop or the priest authorized to investigate these situations. It is important to remember that superstition about demonic forces and what they are capable of must be dispelled.

What Is an Exorcism?

The goal of the devil is the conquest of civilization. God is the one who gives structure and order to society. The devil wants to destroy God's plan for humanity and to replace it with his own. His first attempt was in the Garden of Eden when he convinced Adam and Eve to act contrary to God's command not to eat of the fruit of the tree of the knowledge of good and evil. He continues this activity in the world today, and to combat him, the Church uses the ministry of exorcism.

An exorcism is a specific form of prayer that the Church utilizes to disrupt the devil's activity and to help those who have fallen under his power. The Catechism of the Catholic Church states, "When the Church asks publicly and authoritatively in the name of Jesus Christ that a person or object be protected against the power of the Evil One and withdrawn from his dominion, it is called *exorcism*" (1673).

Many people today may have some notion of what the

word 'exorcism' means based on their own research or a definition that has been shaped by modern culture. There is a great fascination today with the devil, evil spirits, exorcism, magic, witchcraft, and paranormal activity. We cannot seem to get enough, and this is reflected in the popularity of movies, television shows, news articles, and the use of the internet.

The beginning of the renewed fascination with exorcism can be attributed to the movie, *The Exorcist*, produced by William Peter Blatty and released in December of 1973. This film thrust into the forefront the reality of the devil and the ministry of exorcism. The interesting thing about all the available information regarding exorcism is that its main goal is to sensationalize and to create a fascination with evil. Exorcists will tell you that if you are going to give a talk on God, about twenty people will show up. However, if you are going to talk about the devil, two hundred people will show up. People always seem to be more interested in what the devil is trying to do. In contrast, in the ministry of exorcism, the focus is always on what God is doing to help the person who is afflicted by evil.

The word *exorcism* comes from the Greek word *exorkismos* and is a term that signifies an insistent request manifested before God or directed against demons. Literally, to exorcize means to bind with an oath. At its very core exorcism is prayer. It is a prayer that shows the afflicted the face of God. It is an act of mercy that unleashes God's love against the attacks of the devil, bringing healing and peace to those afflicted by the evil one, allowing them to be reconciled to God. It is a ministry of compassion. It is a ministry of charity. It is a ministry of mercy. The Church does not charge any fee to help people overcome the demonic in their lives. It is not a hobby or a game or something done for entertainment. It is a struggle against Satan that relies on the power of Jesus Christ and the authority he gave to his Church.

When God is being requested to expel a demon, it is called a supplicating or minor exorcism. Prayers for deliverance would fall under this category. When the demon or evil spirits are being addressed, it is called an imperative or major exorcism. The distinction is that major exorcisms are only performed in cases of true demonic possession. Minor exorcisms are used to help a person to overcome the influence of evil and sin in their life.

Catholic belief holds that anyone may say a minor prayer of exorcism on behalf of someone else, since it is a prayer directed to God who is asked to bring relief to the person experiencing evil in their life. Anyone can pray. However, a major exorcism, as an official liturgical rite of the Catholic Church, is reserved to the priest who has been authorized to perform this ministry by his bishop. The 1983 Code of Canon Law for the Western Church states, "No one can perform exorcisms legitimately upon the possessed unless he has obtained special and express permission from the local ordinary. The local ordinary is to give this permission only to a presbyter who has piety, knowledge, prudence, and integrity of life" (Canon 1172). In most cases the term 'local ordinary' refers to the diocesan bishop.

A balanced approach to this ministry is important, as well as being grounded in Scripture and the sacramental life of the Church. I believe that the priest appointed to be the exorcist needs to have a strong priestly identity, be at ease in his priesthood, and not do this ministry full time. It is good to balance this ministry with pastoring a parish and being involved in the sacramental lives of the faithful. I say this because battling the forces of evil can be spiritually, mentally, and physically draining. Parish life can help the exorcist to constantly renew himself. Another good quality is possessing a sense of humor. Being able to laugh can help dissipate the stress that comes from this ministry.

I said earlier there is no cost to receive an exorcism. That is unequivocally true. Yet there is the joke that says if you do not pay for your exorcism you will get repossessed! It is sad that there are people who will prey on people's spiritual brokenness and suffering for monetary gain. Several years ago, I was contacted by a man in another state who told me he was possessed. Listening to his story, I determined this was not the case. I recommended counseling and offered to help him find a therapist. Insistent that this was something truly demonic, he contacted someone who identified as a professional exorcist. He called me back to say that he was told he was possessed by five demons and he would have to pay $1500 each to have them cast out.

The ritual itself, *Exorcisms and Related Supplications*, says that the priest who is appointed to this ministry is one who "has been specifically prepared for this office."[1] Preparation for the office is done primarily through the apprenticeship model, whereby the newly appointed exorcist will work under a more seasoned exorcist. The Church has also created programs, workshops, and associations to help the exorcist to better understand how to help those who reach out to him.

The local bishop has the final say on all matters as they pertain to exorcism. As a successor to the Apostles, the bishop is the exorcist in his diocese and the one whom the Holy Spirit has given the governing power to assess matters related to demonic activity. At his discretion, a bishop may bestow this charism on one or more of his priests. He may appoint any priest on a case by case basis, or he may appoint a priest on a stable basis to perform this ministry. It is important to note that exorcists are appointed to function only in their respective dioceses and only under the direction of their bishop. They are not appointed for the universal Church and

[1] *The Roman Ritual: Exorcisms and Related Supplications* [English Translation According to the Typical Edition, For Use in the Diocese of the United States of America, Approved by the United States Conference of Catholic Bishops and Confirmed by the Apostolic See] (Washington, DC: International Commission on English in the Liturgy Corporation, 2017), 13.

they do not act independent of their bishop. I can assist in another diocese either by weighing in on a case or performing an actual exorcism only if requested by that local bishop. The authority of a bishop in his own diocese must always be respected, and when it is not it only results in trouble.

Early in this ministry, I recall the story of a priest from another diocese who came into the Archdiocese of Indianapolis to perform an exorcism without my bishop's permission. During the rite, the demon manifested and mocked him saying, "Who are you? You have no authority over us. We recognize the authority of the local bishop as a successor to the Apostles. But you, you are nobody. You have no authority to give commands to us. We will not listen to what you tell us." He quickly recognized the error of his ways and sought the proper delegation from the Archbishop of Indianapolis. Since he was already working with the afflicted person, he was granted permission to do the exorcism, but only under my supervision and with my involvement in the case. It proved to be a good educational experience for me as I continued to grow in this ministry.

The role of the exorcist is to investigate cases of alleged demonic activity and determine if the official rite of the Church needs to be utilized. However, most people who contact me have already self-diagnosed. They have reached their own conclusion that they or a loved one is possessed and need an exorcism. The Church makes it clear that she is the one who will make this determination. I cannot tell you the number of people who get angry and upset with me when I don't accept their conclusion that they are possessed. There is no such thing as an emergency exorcism. It cannot be rushed. It involves a process. In my experience, those who are not willing to follow the guidance and direction that the Church has laid out are not really dealing with the demonic. After all, if one genuinely believes they are possessed I think they would be ready and willing to do whatever is prescribed.

Even with this said, it should be stated that the exorcist must not be the first line of defense for someone who believes they are dealing with the demonic. Exorcists should only see those who truly need their help. Many people who believe they need to see an exorcist can have most of their problems resolved by their parish priest. Every priest should have an openness and a sensitivity to the reality of evil present in the lives of the faithful. He should be the first contact, using discernment to listen to the person, to assess where they are spiritually, to pray with them, to offer them a blessing, to hear their confession, and if need be to contact the exorcist in his diocese. Afflictions attributed to the evil one should be seen in the broader scope of overall pastoral care, and this is best provided at the parish level.

It would be unrealistic to think that an exorcist could provide long-term spiritual care for all those who come to him for exorcism. A good analogy for the local priest and exorcist working together would be one's family doctor and a specialist in a certain field of medicine. If one goes to their family doctor for severe headaches, they may be referred to a neurologist for more detailed care. Once the specialist has addressed the problem, the person is returned to their family doctor for on-going care. Using this example, a person who is suffering demonic attacks goes to see their local priest who then refers them to the exorcist. Once the exorcist works with the person, they are sent back to their parish priest for on-going pastoral care.

The role of the local priest in being well formed and informed about how to help people in their fight against evil is essential; because it is in the local parish where people experience the sacramental life of the Church. And when it comes to the sacraments and defeating the devil, the number one weapon in our arsenal is the Sacrament of Penance. The importance of going to confession cannot be overstated. Fr. Gabriele Amorth, the former chief exorcist of Rome who died in 2016, said that the place to begin with anyone who believes they are up against the forces of evil is for that person to make a good confession. He says, "The more a person confesses, the more he is aware of his defects; the less he confesses, the less he sees them."[2]

When we confess our sins, we place them in the hands of God, and once we have given them over to God, the devil may

---

[2]   Amorth, *My Battle Against Satan*, 81.

no longer use them against us. Taking ownership of our sinful acts by confessing them deprives the devil of a foothold in our lives. If that demonic foothold is of a more severe nature, then this is where the Rite of Exorcism comes into play. Demons have power. They can only be defeated by power. The power that defeats them is the power of God. In an exorcism, the exorcist is a tool that God uses to demonstrate his power over the demonic and to bring about liberation for the one held in the grip of the devil.

PRACTICAL INSIGHT FROM THE GOSPEL OF MARK

Much can be learned from the Gospel of Mark about the ministry of exorcism. The fact that it is the first of the Gospels to be written and the author chose to put a strong emphasis on the practice of exorcism speaks to just how important it is. In Mark, there are four accounts of Jesus performing exorcisms: (1) The Man with an Unclean Spirit, (2) Jesus Heals the Gersasene Demoniac, (3) The Syrophoenician Woman's Faith, and (4) The Healing of a Boy with a Mute Spirit.

By looking at these biblical accounts, we learn firsthand what Jesus did when he encountered demons. His approach to combatting Satan and his angels must be the one that we imitate because from it we learn that exorcisms are about the authority of Jesus Christ, they heal the brokenness in people's lives, they are available to Catholics and non-Catholics, and faith is the essential ingredient in their efficacy.

The Man with an Unclean Spirit (Mark 1:21–28)

> And they went into Capernaum; and immediately
> on the sabbath he entered the synagogue and taught.
> And they were astonished at his teaching, for he
> taught them as one who had authority, and not as
> the scribes. And immediately there was in their syna-
> gogue a man with an unclean spirit; and he cried out,
> "What have you to do with us, Jesus of Nazareth?
> Have you come to destroy us? I know who you are,
> the Holy One of God." But Jesus rebuked him, saying,
> "Be silent, and come out of him!" And the unclean
> spirit, convulsing him and crying with a loud voice,
> came out of him. And they were all amazed, so that
> they questioned among themselves, saying, "What is
> this? A new teaching! With authority he commands
> even the unclean spirits, and they obey him." And at
> once his fame spread everywhere throughout all the
> surrounding region of Galilee.

The key element of an exorcism found in this passage is the
authority to command unclean spirits in the name of Jesus
Christ. Jesus spoke with authority when he commanded demons to depart from their victim, and exorcists must speak
with the same authority and conviction. There must be no fear
or hesitation in the voice of the exorcist when he confronts a
demon because he is speaking, not on his own authority but,

on the authority that comes from Jesus Christ. The demon will pick up on any doubt or hesitation on the part of the exorcist and try to use it for its own advantage. The exorcist must always have the upper hand during an exorcism, and this is found in the authority that Jesus gave the Church.

This account also gives us some insight into the nature and character of demons:

+ Demons understand the identity of Jesus. "The Holy One of God" (1:24).

+ Demons know Jesus' mission. "Have you come to destroy us?" (1:24).

+ Demons act in clusters. When a person is possessed, it is normally the case that it is not just one but many demons with one exercising some power or control over the others. We are told the man was possessed by an unclean spirt—in the singular, but immediately the demon speaks in the plural—'us' on two occasions and then goes back to speaking in the singular—'I' (Mark 1:24).

+ Demons recognize the authority of Jesus. "Be silent, and come out of him" (1:26). There is no background information provided in this account as to what the entry point may have been for the unclean spirit to possess this man. Jesus as the Holy One of God would have been able to fully understand the situation. However, for the exorcist to properly use the authority given to him by the Church, he must come to a level of understanding of how the demon entered into a person. Knowing the entry point will give him the moral certitude needed to proceed with an exorcism.

• Demons must obey the authority of Jesus. "And the unclean spirit, convulsing him and crying with a loud voice, came out of him" (1:26).

Jesus Heals the Gerasene Demoniac
(Mark 5:1–20)

They came to the other side of the sea, to the country of the Gerasenes. And when he had come out of the boat, there met him out of the tombs a man with an unclean spirit, who lived among the tombs; and no one could bind him any more, even with a chain; for he had often been bound with shackles and chains, but the chains he wrenched apart, and the shackles he broke in pieces; and no one had the strength to subdue him. Night and day among the tombs and on the mountains he was always crying out, and bruising himself with stones. And when he saw Jesus from afar, he ran and worshiped him; and crying out with a loud voice, he said, "What have you to do with me, Jesus, Son of the Most High God? I adjure you by God, do not torment me." For he had said to him, "Come out of the man, you unclean spirit!" And Jesus asked him, "What is your name?" He replied, "My name is Legion; for we are many." And he begged him eagerly not to send them out of the country. Now a great herd of swine was feeding there on the hillside; and they begged him, "Send us to the swine, let us enter them." So he gave them leave. And the unclean spirits came out, and entered the swine; and the herd, numbering about two thousand, rushed down the steep bank into the sea, and were drowned in the sea. The herdsmen fled, and told it in the city and in the country. And people came to see what it was that had happened. And they came to Jesus, and saw the demoniac sitting there, clothed and in his right mind, the man who had had the legion; and they were afraid. And those who had seen it told what had happened to the demoniac and to the swine. And they began to beg Jesus to depart from their neighborhood. And as he was getting into the boat, the man who had been possessed with demons begged him that he might be with him. But he refused, and said to him, "Go home to your friends, and tell them how much the Lord has done for you, and how he has had mercy on you." And he went away and began to proclaim in the Decapolis how much Jesus had done for him; and all men marveled.

The key element of exorcism found in this passage is that of healing the brokenness in our lives that can be an entry point for the demonic. Demons will attempt to enter the brokenness and dysfunction in our lives to try to fracture and break us even more. Jesus is the one who has the power to bring the broken pieces of our lives together making us whole and complete. This is what he did with the Gerasene Demoniac. Here are some important things we learn from this passage:

+ The man with the unclean spirit was in isolation and "lived among the tombs" (5:3). Demons thrive on isolating us from the support we receive from community.
+ One who is possessed exhibits extraordinary human strength. "The chains he wrenched apart, and the shackles he broke into pieces" (5:4). This is one of the four signs mentioned in the Rite of Exorcism.
+ Demons recognize Jesus' identity, "What have you to do with me, Jesus, Son of the Most High God?" (5:7).
+ When demons reveal their name, they are submitting to the power and authority of Jesus. "And Jesus asked him, 'What is your name?'" (5:9). This question was included in the rite from the year 1614 but is not included in the rite that was promulgated in 1998.
+ It is rarely a case of just one demon when someone is possessed. "My name is Legion; for we are many" (5:9). In this specific case, there were about 2000 demons!

"And the herd, numbering about two thousand, rushed down the steep bank into the sea, and were drowned in the sea" (5:13).

- It is possible for animals to be possessed. "And the unclean spirits came out, and entered the swine" (5:13).
- Exorcisms require people to see the power of God at work and to enter into a relationship with him. People who do not want to submit to Jesus will either walk away from their faith or ask Jesus to leave. "And they began to beg Jesus to depart from their neighborhood" (5:17).
- Jesus respects our free will. He does not force himself on us. When he is asked to leave, we are told he got "into the boat" (5:18).
- Jesus restores us to right relationships. The man who is now free from Legion desires to come with Jesus but is told to "Go home to your friends" (5:20). Rarely, if ever, does Jesus tell someone not to follow him. What we learn from the ending of this passage is that Jesus takes a man living among the dead in the tombs and places him among the living, his friends. Jesus takes the man from isolation and places him within community. Jesus heals the brokenness that was the entry point for the demonic, into this man's life, and gives him a new future full of hope. Exorcisms provide this same benefit today.

THE SYROPHOENICIAN WOMAN'S FAITH
(MARK 7:24–30)

And from there he arose and went away to the region of Tyre and Sidon. And he entered a house, and would not have any one know it; yet he could not be hidden. But immediately a woman, whose little daughter was possessed by an unclean spirit, heard of him, and came and fell down at his feet. Now the woman was a Greek, a Syrophoenician by birth. And she begged him to cast the demon out of her daughter. And he said to her, "Let the children first be fed, for it is not right to take the children's bread and throw it to the dogs." But she answered him, "Yes, Lord; yet even the dogs under the table eat the children's crumbs." And he said to her, "For this saying you may go your way; the demon has left your daughter." And she went home, and found the child lying in bed, and the demon gone.

The key ingredient about exorcisms from this biblical account is that exorcism is a ministry of charity open to all God's children. The Church must demonstrate an acceptance of all people who approach her requesting an exorcism. Here are some key details from this passage:

+ An exorcism may not be performed on someone against their will. However, one who has authority over another, such as a parent, can request an exorcism on their behalf. "And she begged him to cast the demon out of her daughter" (7:26).

+ Exorcisms require a profession of faith because it is not what the exorcist is doing per se, but what God is accomplishing through this prayer of the Church. When an exorcist works with someone who is not Catholic, what he looks for in the person asking for help is a belief in the power of God. The exorcist must never be viewed as a wizard performing some sort of magical rite. Jesus' words to the woman can seem harsh, but by his words he presents her with the opportunity to articulate her belief in what God is able to accomplish. "Let the children first be fed, for it is not right to take the children's bread and throw it to the dogs" (7:27).

+ Exorcisms can take place from a distance. In this case the demon was expelled from the girl without Jesus being present. "And she went home, and found the child lying in bed, and the demon gone" (7:30).

THE HEALING OF A BOY WITH A MUTE SPIRIT (MARK 9:14–29)

And when they came to the disciples, they saw a great crowd about them, and scribes arguing with them. And immediately all the crowd, when they saw him, were greatly amazed, and ran up to him and greeted him. And he asked them, "What are you discussing with them?" And one of the crowd answered him, "Teacher, I brought my son to you, for he has a mute spirit; and whenever it seizes him, it dashes him down; and he foams and grinds his teeth and becomes rigid; and I asked your disciples to cast it out, and they were not able." And he answered them, "O faithless generation, how long am I to be with you? How long am I to bear with you? Bring him to me." And they brought the boy to him; and when the spirit saw him, immediately it convulsed the boy, and he fell on the ground and rolled about, foaming at the mouth. And Jesus asked his father, "How long has he done this?" And he said, "From childhood. And it has often cast him into the fire and into the water, to destroy him; but if you can do anything, have pity on us and help us." And Jesus said to him, "If you can! All things are possible to him who believes." Immediately the father of the child cried out and said, "I believe; help my unbelief!" And when Jesus saw that a crowd came running together, he rebuked the unclean spirit, saying to it, "You mute and deaf spirit, I command you, come out of him, and never enter him again." And after crying out and convulsing him terribly, it came out, and the boy was like a corpse; so that most of them said, "He is dead." But Jesus took him by the hand and lifted him up, and he arose. And when he had entered the house, his disciples asked him privately, "Why could we not cast it out?" And he said to them, "This kind cannot be driven out by anything but prayer and fasting."

The key component we learn from this passage is the importance of faith. Jesus demonstrates that he is more concerned about the father's lack of faith as opposed to the boy who is convulsing on the ground. When an exorcist is working with someone, it is not simply a matter of casting the evil out, it is also about bringing God in. Therefore, the person seeking the help of the Church must be open to recommitting themselves to their faith in Jesus Christ. Perhaps they have walked away from Jesus or they must be willing to come to a relationship with him for the very first time. Here are some important points about exorcism we learn from this passage:

+ Jesus makes a distinction between physical ailments and those caused by demonic possession. "For he has a mute spirit" (9:17).
+ There are signs of demonic possession that include foaming at the mouth, the grinding of teeth, and the body becoming rigid (9:18).
+ Not all exorcisms are successful. "I asked your disciples to cast it out, and they were unable" (9:18). God is al-

ways in charge and will determine when a demon will be cast out. We operate on his timing and not our own. This reinforces that in this prayer it is what God is doing and not any perceived power coming from the exorcist.

+ One can be possessed for an extended period of time. In this case, the boy was possessed "from childhood" (9:21).

+ Demons' main purpose is to destroy us. "And it has often cast him into the fire and into the water, to destroy him" (9:22).

+ Exorcisms are a form of evangelization because they can help those who are concerned for the welfare of their loved ones who are possessed to grow in faith. "I believe; help my unbelief" (9:24).

+ When demons are cast out of the one they are afflicting, they always cry out in pain. "And after crying out and convulsing him terribly, it came out" (9:26). Exorcists can know with certainty that a demon has truly been cast out and is not merely giving the illusion that it is gone when there is a shriek or scream.

+ The exorcist must be properly prepared. In this particular case, prayer and fasting were essential ingredients. "This kind cannot be driven out by anything but prayer and fasting" (9:29).

What we learn from these four biblical accounts of exorcism is that Jesus is the one who guides the process and sets the standards for how to confront Satan and his angels. Following the proper protocol established by Jesus and understanding what demons are capable of ensures that exorcisms will always be successful and achieve their purpose of wresting one from the domain and power of the devil and placing them in the domain and grace of God.

THE RITE OF EXORCISM

The Catholic Church does not have a monopoly on the practice of exorcism. However, since it is a liturgical rite that falls under the Congregation for Divine Worship and the Discipline of the Sacraments, there is a prescribed way for it to be done. The Second Vatican Council (1962–1965) called for all liturgical rites to be revised. The Rite of Exorcism was the last of the liturgical rites to be revised after the Council and was promulgated in 1998. This major revision of the Rite of Exorcism was an extensive undertaking, the likes of which had not taken place since the year 1614. It is amazing to think that from 1614 to 1998—384 years, the rite remained virtually unchanged. This Latin text was published in 1999 under the title, *De Exorcismis et Supplicationibus Quibusdam*, and later revised in 2004 and again in 2005. The English translation, *Exorcisms and Related Supplications*, was issued in 2016.

One of the things that stands out in the new rite is that

along with the revision of the major Rite of Exorcism, to be performed on a possessed person, there are supplication or minor exorcism prayers. These prayers are directed to God who is asked to bring relief into the life of the one who is being afflicted by the evil one. By adding these prayers, the Church wanted to place the pastoral care of those who were being afflicted by the extraordinary activity of the devil in the hands of every parish priest. The new rite also includes the Exorcism Prayers of Pope Leo XIII. Additionally, there are prayers which may be recited privately by the faithful in their own struggle against evil. Currently, these prayers are now available in a separate resource to be used by the general public on their own behalf.

In the Rite of Exorcism, the Church reenacts Christ's victory over Satan by literally throwing into the face of the demon the aspects of the Christian faith the devil has rejected. These aspects, including the use of holy water and a crucifix, are incorporated into the rite and it is important for people to know how exorcism works. The exorcist is not a wizard using magic and props. He is a representative of the Church who uses tangible things to make real the aspects of our Christian faith. During an exorcism, he calls upon the power of Jesus Christ and speaks with the authority found in his name.

There is a detailed exorcism performed by St. Paul found in the Acts of the Apostles: "As we were going to the place of prayer, we were met by a slave girl who had a spirit of divination and brought her owners much gain by sooth-saying. She followed Paul and us, crying, 'These men are servants of the Most High God, who proclaim to you the way of salvation.' And this she did for many days. But Paul was annoyed, and turned and said to the spirit, 'I charge you in the name of Jesus Christ to come out of her.' And it came out that very hour" (16:16–18). Based on this biblical account, it can be said that an exorcism is a command given to a demon in the name of Jesus Christ ordering it to leave its victim.

Before celebrating the rite, I will prepare myself by spending time in prayer, fasting, going to confession, and celebrating Mass. Exorcists need to be in a state of grace be-cause they face real dangers from the battles they engage in against Satan and his angels. Demons do not want to depart from their victims and will do anything and everything to hold on. There are examples of demons who manifest and be-gin spouting out the sins of the exorcist in order to humiliate him and make him feel inadequate in this battle. The devil knows who is working to defeat him and will do everything in his power to distract the exorcist so that he can disrupt the prayer of the Church and continue his hold on the one who is afflicted.

The exorcist is always the one in charge of this prayer. After my personal preparations, I then determine where the exorcism is to take place. Exorcisms are always performed in a sacred space such as a church or chapel where there is a crucifix and an image of the Blessed Virgin Mary. They are never performed in an abandoned house, on a dead-end street, at midnight, during a thunderstorm. That might make for a good movie, but it is not reality. The devil does not get to choose where he will be defeated. The Church herself makes that determination.

I then decide who will be present. In addition to myself and the one who is possessed, there will be a family member or friend and those who are invited to pray during the rite. These are people who know the importance of not acting independent of the exorcist's direction by doing such things as looking into the eyes of the demon, interrupting the exorcism, or reciting the prayers along with the exorcist. All these people must prepare themselves beforehand so as not to be the weak link the demon uses to continue to lay siege to his victim. On numerous occasions during an exorcism, I have witnessed the demon manifest and then begin fixating his eyes on the others in the room trying to determine whom he can rattle the most. The manifestations are meant to instill fear and to cause those present to focus on what the demon is doing to show his power, rather than focusing on the power of God made evident through the Rite of Exorcism. Once a deacon was assisting me and the demon manifested and seeing the deacon look him in the eye, told him in these or similar words, "You think you're so smart. You're nothing but a bag of excrement!"

People are not invited to be part of an exorcism out of a sense of curiosity but to be active participants in this particular prayer of the Church. There is no such thing as exorcism tourism. Confidentiality on the part of those present is crucial. The rite itself states that, "In no way may any opportunity be given to any of the media of social communication while the Exorcism is taking place, or even before the Exorcism takes place, and when it has been performed the Exorcist and those present, observing due discretion, should not divulge information about it."[1] People always say if an exorcism was more public by being recorded and shown to a larger audience it would have a great impact on those who doubt the devil's existence. The reason for the privacy of the celebration of the rite is to protect the dignity of the person and not allow them to become an object of study or curiosity.

When I am ready to begin, I put on a purple stole as a sign of my priestly office, say a prayer asking God to strengthen me in my attack against this evil spirit, and have with me holy water and a crucifix. These things are important tools against the devil, as the use of blessed religious objects finds its basis in the following scriptural account: "And God did extraordinary miracles by the hands of Paul, so that handkerchiefs or aprons were carried away from his body to the sick, and diseases left them and the evil spirits came out of them" (Acts 19:11–12).

[1] *The Roman Ritual: Exorcisms and Related Supplications*, 19.

The entire rite is divided into the following parts, not including the private preparations of the exorcist himself:

+ The sprinkling of holy water which recalls the Sacrament of Baptism and the fact that one is the temple of God. In Baptism, one dies to self and puts on Jesus Christ. The rite begins with the blessing with holy water to say to the devil, this person does not belong to you. They belong to God.

+ The Litany of the Saints, calling upon the Blessed Virgin Mary, the angels, and the Communion of Saints to be present as the Church invokes the mercy of God. A major exorcism is a public prayer of the Church that includes our Blessed Mother, the Angelic Choirs, and the countless holy men and women down through the ages of the Church.

+ The recitation of one or several of the Psalms. The devil is defeated through the Word of God and the Psalms are powerful expressions of God's love for humanity.

+ The proclamation of the Gospel that signifies the presence of Christ. The Gospels are the words of Jesus himself. Catholics stand at Mass when the Gospel is proclaimed in recognition that Jesus is present in his Word. The Word of God is a powerful tool used to defeat the devil.

+ Invoking the power of the Holy Spirit through the laying on of hands and breathing upon the face of the afflicted person. Whenever the Holy Spirit is present, an unclean spirit cannot remain. This action recalls Jesus breathing upon his disciples and conferring on them the Holy Spirit. Strengthened by the Spirit, they let go of their fear, leaving the locked room where they were and went and proclaimed the Gospel (John 20:19–23).

+ The Profession of Faith or the renewal of the baptismal promises, followed by the Lord's Prayer. By renewing their commitment to Jesus Christ, the person is demonstrating the use of their free will to renounce Satan by stating that which they believe. The recitation of the Lord's Prayer allows the person to acknowledge God as their Father and the desire to be liberated from the evil one.

+ The afflicted person is shown a Crucifix and the Sign of the Cross is made over the person. The devil is made to realize that the moment of his perceived victory is actually the moment of his defeat. Christ dying on the Cross was not a sign of weakness but one of victory and triumph over the devil. The Cross is one of the most powerful signs in the Christian faith.

+ A supplicating prayer is said, by which God is asked to bring relief into the life of the one who is suffering. God is the one who is the Great Liberator and he is always addressed before the demon.

+ This is followed by an imperative or major exorcism, by which the devil, in the name of Jesus Christ, is commanded to depart from the one who is afflicted.[2]

Depending on the severity of the demonic possession, the rite may have to be prayed repeatedly over an extended period of time, sometimes months and even years. The priest who trained me suggested that each session should last approximately thirty to sixty minutes with follow up sessions scheduled until the demonic presence is fully gone. We might wonder why the rite must be prayed over and over again and not just once. After all, Jesus never had to have a follow up session with anyone from whom he cast out demons. If an exorcism seems ineffective, one must consider the strength and character of the demon and the fact that the afflicted person may not be properly prepared to receive liberation. The desire to be freed from suffering is not the same as wanting to be free from the demon. There must be a desire to turn from sin and to have a relationship with Jesus Christ. Fr. Gabriele Amorth reminds us that every exorcism session always provides a benefit even if the person fails to receive total liberation. Everything happens according to God's timing which is "always oriented toward eternal life."[3]

It has been my experience that demons seem to have a

2   *The Roman Ritual: Exorcisms and Related Supplications*, 21–30.
3   Amorth, *My Battle Against Satan*, 36.

more powerful hold on those who have heard the Good News of Jesus Christ but who have now turned a deaf ear to it. The greater presence of the demonic in the world today, along with the call for more exorcisms, is because too many people have walked away from their relationship with Jesus Christ. In some of the more severe cases of demonic possession, the exorcist may choose to use the older rite of the Church. Some exorcists find these prayers richer in content and expression. Therefore, in response to this, on April 30, 2011 the Congregation for Divine Worship and the Discipline of the Sacraments gave permission to all priests who are stably appointed exorcists to use, at their discretion, whichever of the rites of exorcism they find to be more beneficial. The most important thing to remember with the various rites is that they are the prayer of the Church. Therefore, they are all efficacious in combatting the devil. I find it a bit troubling when there are disagreements among exorcists about which of the various rites of the Church are most effective. I once heard an exorcist say that when he was performing an exorcism the demon told him that he did not like the new rite of 1998 and even laughed that he could not be cast out with that translation. Since the devil is the father of all lies, I find it best not to pay attention to what any demon has to say. I prefer to always focus on the prayer of the Church and what God is doing, as opposed to the attempts of the devil to sow disharmony and division among the priests who are fighting against him.

Once during an exorcism, the manifesting demon gave the impression that it had been cast out. It remarked to me, "You can stop praying now. Thank you so much for what you have done here today. Stop praying. I feel so much better now. Stop praying. You have been so helpful. Stop praying." Knowing that the demon was trying to deceive me, I blessed the person again with holy water and the demon screamed at me, "I said you can stop praying!" An exorcist should never allow a demon to take control of the situation by paying more attention to the words of the demon than to the words of the Church.

Playing the Devil's Game

The Bible presents specific instructions on how to gain victory over the devil. St. Paul admonishes us to "give no opportunity to the devil" (Eph 4:27). St. Peter teaches us, "Be sober, be watchful. Your adversary the devil prowls around like a roaring lion, seeking some one to devour. Resist him, firm in your faith" (1 Pet 5:8–9a). And St. James says, "Submit yourselves therefore to God. Resist the devil and he will flee from you" (Jas 4:7). The sad truth is that far too many people are giving the devil an opportunity. They are not being sober and watchful in their faith. And they are certainly not resisting him. Indeed, it is my firm conviction that the devil has not upped his game against humanity. Rather, more people are demonstrating a willingness to play his game.

We build our eternal destiny by the choices we make. St. Athanasius teaches us that the human person was created to move according to virtue, but when we abuse our freedom of choice, we move in the wrong direction.[1] We are living in a unique moment of human history where many people are choosing to move in the wrong direction. Christianity is being replaced with demonic doctrines and practices that are drawing so many people away from the path to the tree of life. Falling for the devil's falsehoods, they have lost their focus on eternal heavenly life and are looking at nothing more than what this temporary earthly life can give.

The key ingredient in defeating the devil is faith. "The more a person lives by faith, the more he is impervious to the devil's attacks: faith is a fortress that protects man from his onslaughts and that is why he endeavors to bring the believer out of the fortress by dazzling him with a host of illusory enticements, as would a conjurer, and by tempting him to rely on something more sensational than pure faith."[2] Abandoning our faith and allowing ourselves to be enticed by the devil is certainly not something unique to our time. St. Paul in writing to Timothy says, "For the time is coming when people will not endure sound teaching, but having itching ears they will accumulate for themselves teachers to suit their own likings, and will turn away from listening to the truth and wander into myths" (2 Tim 4:3–4).

In the fifteen years that I have been an exorcist, I have

---

[1] Athanasius, *Against the Heathens* (Middletown, DE: Beloved Publishing, 2014).
[2] Suenens, *Renewal and the Powers of Darkness*, 34.

identified eight major ways that I believe people can become vulnerable to playing the devil's game. Some create this opening directly and others do it indirectly. Some play the devil's game directly when they actively engage in activities that are meant to cultivate a relationship with evil spirits—they know what they are doing is wrong, but they choose to do it any way. Others play the devil's game indirectly when they engage in activities they perceive to be fun and entertaining, but in reality create a connection with evil spirits. There are countless ways that people can create an entry point for evil into their lives. I want to share with you the eight major ways that I have witnessed over the years.

1. The World of the Occult

The word "occult" comes from the Latin *occultus*, meaning hidden or secret. Its basic principle is that people want to bypass God. The world of the occult is extremely complex and diverse. It is expressed in various ways by such things as superstition, idolatry, and divination, but ultimately falls under the heading of magic. All magic is inherently evil and very dangerous because it has its origin in "the dominion of darkness" (Col 1:13). As such, it is addressed extensively in the Catechism of the Catholic Church.[3] By magic I am not

---

[3] CCC, 2110–2117.

speaking of an illusionist who plays tricks on our eyes by making something seem to disappear, but magic in the true sense of the word whereby there is a diabolical component. The devil is the source of power behind all magic. It must always be avoided because "what is evil in nature can never produce good."[4] Let me say a little more about this.

People who go to see psychics and mediums looking for answers to life's problems need to understand they are turning to the devil and his power for help. The power they demonstrate does not originate from them because it is contrary to human nature. We must realize that a non-material world does exist with non-material beings; namely, demons. These entities are the source of the power and knowledge displayed through the use of astrology, palm readings, tea leaf reading, tarot cards, Spiritism (séances and automatic writing), pendulums, Santeria, Voodoo, potions, herbs, amulets, and crystals. All these practices are condemned for they are a form of idolatry that violates the first of the Ten Commandments where God says, "You shall have no other gods before me" (Exod 20:3). In other words, nothing must ever be elevated above God's rightful place in our lives, and when we turn to the tools of the trade of psychics and mediums, we are putting something in the place of God. This law of God is reinforced in the Book of Leviticus where we are told, "Do not turn to mediums or wizards; do not seek them out, to be

---

[4] Athanasius, *Against the Heathens*, 15.

defiled by them. I am the Lord your God" (19:31). The Book
of Deuteronomy takes it a step further saying, "There shall
not be found among you . . . any one who practices divination,
a soothsayer, or an augur, or a sorcerer, or a charmer, or a medium, or a wizard, or a necromancer. For whoever does these
things is an abomination to the Lord" (18:10–12).

Some psychics and mediums know that the power operating through them is coming from an evil spirit. Others
have been duped by evil spirits into believing the power is
coming directly from them. The devil knows what he is plot-
ting against someone and will use psychics and mediums in
order to manipulate people for his own purposes. We need to
be wary of them since they may use Christian symbols, such
as a crucifix or an image of the Blessed Mother, in order to
lure people in by giving them a false sense of security that
there is nothing wrong with what they are doing. The First
Letter of John makes it very clear that "many false prophets
have gone out into the world" (4:1), and "every spirit which
does not confess Jesus is not of God" (4:3). The devil has
every motivation to get us to engage in practices that break
the First Commandment.

When people allow themselves to be duped by psychics
and mediums, the result is the establishment of a relationship between the person and the forces of evil. At first there
are thrills and fascinations with what the person is hearing
through the psychic or medium, but eventually the demon-

ic presence will reveal itself and the person's life will begin to unravel. When the devil gives something, he will expect something in return. When power is gained, and special favors granted through the assistance of the devil and his angels, they will expect to be paid in full. The price demanded is our destruction through the loss of our soul. Magic is an effective destructive weapon of the devil due to weak religious convictions. St. John Paul II has said, "The weakening of faith leads to a degeneration into magical practices."[5]

My best advice is to forget about magic and the world of the occult and always turn to God through prayer for the answers we are seeking. The Book of Joshua says it best, "but as for me and my house, we will serve the Lord" (24:15). Blessed Bartolo Longo (1841–1926) is a great intercessor for those caught up in the occult and the world of magic. Growing up in a devout Catholic family he lost his faith while attending university in Naples, Italy. He was drawn into the demonic world of darkness to the extent that he even became a satanic high priest. His family never gave up on him, and through much prayer he returned to the Church and dedicated his life to the Rosary and the Blessed Virgin Mary. He was instrumental in the building of the Shrine of Our Lady of Pompeii just outside Naples. His story is important because it lets us know that although a demon may seem to be victorious in his conquest of

---

[5] Pope St. John Paul II, Apostolic Letter *Novo Millennio Ineunte* (January 6, 2001), § 34.

a person, it is never too late for them to be set free.

Several years ago, I worked with someone who had practiced witchcraft and wanted to renounce it and return to God. During the conversation, a demon manifested and the person ran out of my office and the demon locked itself in a restroom. When I was able to get the door open, the demon was glaring at me with blood dripping from the person's mouth. I then noticed that the blood had been used to draw a pentagram on the mirror in the restroom. The demon was attempting to startle and scare me. Using the prayers of the Church, I was able to take control of the situation and cast the demon out.

2. THE ENTERTAINMENT INDUSTRY

In the world of entertainment, I include things like movies, television shows, literature, board and card games, computer and IT gadgets, horoscopes, ghost hunting, Halloween, and the practice of Yoga and Reiki. People, especially children, are growing up in front of screens filled with demons and monsters. They are playing with card games that can be an introductory rite into the hierarchical world of demons. They are using Ouija boards to ask questions of evil spirits. They are reading books that present evil as something good and promote being a witch or wizard as a position of power. They are consulting their horoscopes and falling into the world of astrology. They are going on ghost hunting excursions where demons are encountered. They are practicing Yoga with positions that are associated with worship of so-called deities. And they are practicing Reiki and its connection with a universal energy that is certainly not the Holy Spirit. There are those who would challenge these statements, saying these things provide some benefit and are harmless. Yes, entertainment and having fun are an important human component, but we must understand there is an underlying catechetical message associated with the things I have listed here. Their main goal is to discreetly move us away from the worship of God and create a connection with the demonic.

I do not see any harm in using game consoles, watching action shows on television, or reading certain types of literature as a form of entertainment or relaxation. However, since the devil acts in very quiet and subtle ways we need to make sure the games we are playing, the shows we are watching, and the books we are reading are not slowly pulling us into the world of darkness. A family once told me they were concerned for their young daughter who was having visions of demons. While visiting the home, I noticed many violent video games and a computer with a screensaver with the face of a demonic creature. I suggested changing the screen and getting rid of the games as a first step in helping their daughter. I was told that the games cost lots of money and were fun, so they had to stay. When I told them they needed to be part of the solution, and it wasn't just about me blessing them and their home with holy water I was asked to leave.

Violent games can be problematic as they can impact how we view other people. Do we see others as created in the image and likeness of God or simply as "things" that need to be eliminated or destroyed? Action shows need to be tempered with our Christian beliefs. If families elect to watch these shows that are often filled with violence, parents should seize the opportunity to discuss with their children why what they are viewing is either consistent or inconsistent with the behavior that God expects of us. When it comes to children and the books they are reading, think about how many of them can recite spells and other magical formulas but struggle to recite the Ten Commandments, the Our Father, or the Hail Mary.

Ghost hunting and its popularity cannot be underestimated. What people need to understand is that for the most part, what is being encountered are evil spirits. Demons do not live at a certain address such as an old house, prison, or hospital. Because they are non-corporeal beings, meaning they have no body, they are neither here nor there. We say they are here or there if they are choosing to act in a location. Ironically, it is the very things ghost hunters are doing to interact with these spirits that causes them to manifest. In many cases, ghost hunters will use psychics and mediums in their endeavors, and when something evil is encountered, contact an exorcist as if he were an exterminator to take care of the problem they created.

Halloween is something that is also problematic when it comes to creating an entry point for the demonic. Its popularity has soared in recent years making it the second most celebrated holiday in the United States, Christmas being the most celebrated. There are Halloween shops that have popped up all over the country with all sorts of ghoulish costumes depicting the likes of demons, ghosts, witches, zombies, and werewolves. There are also many haunted houses, corn mazes, and insane asylums. People need to know that Halloween is a trap the devil uses to lure them into his world of evil. It begins with the desire for fun and entertainment and ends with the glorification of Satan and his angels.

Finally, there are the practices of Yoga and Reiki that have become extremely popular. Although these can rightly be included under occult practices, I have elected to place it under the heading of entertainment because many people who practice these alternative therapies may not fully understand the risk to which they are exposing themselves. They may say they do it for the benefit of physical exercise, or one's spiritual health, but then get pulled into a worldview that is not compatible with Christianity. There have been attempts to put a Christian spin on these practices, but neither Yoga nor

Reiki can be Christianized. Fr. Gabriele Amorth warns that Yoga is unacceptable to Christians saying that, along with other Eastern methods of meditation, "Often these apparently innocent practices can bring about hallucinations and schizophrenic conditions."[6] In regards to Reiki, the United States Conference of Catholic Bishops states that, "A Catholic who puts his or her trust in Reiki would be operating in the realm of superstition" and then adds, "Superstition corrupts one's worship of God by turning one's religious feelings and practices in a false direction."[7]

The real danger with the world of entertainment is that it can cause us to take our eyes off God and fall into the world of darkness. "When one sets aside God . . . traps spring up everywhere, and it becomes tragically certain that a door will be opened for the Prince of Evil. The demon, as God's mimic, has his sacramentals: drugs, alcohol, illicit sex, alternative religious practices, magic, charms, et cetera."[8] As the Letter to the Hebrews reminds us, "Jesus Christ is the same yesterday and today and for ever. Do not be led away by diverse and strange teachings" (13:8–9).

---

6   Gabriele Amorth, *An Exorcist Tells His Story* (San Francisco, CA: Ignatius Press, 1999), 54.
7   USCCB Committee on Doctrine, *Guidelines for Evaluating Reiki as an Alternative Therapy* (March 25, 2009), 11.
8   Amorth, *My Battle Against Satan*, 125.

3. CURSE

A curse is the opposite of a blessing. When someone or something is blessed, it is commended to God. When something is cursed, it is commended to the devil. The priest will bless us at the end of Mass, parents give their children a blessing, when someone sneezes we say, "God bless you." Items are also blessed to give them a sacred purpose such as holy water, a statue, or a medal. Blessings are good because they make us more aware of the presence of God. Curses, on the other hand, are extremely dangerous because their main goal is to get us to focus on the presence of the demonic. To curse means to do harm to another with the help of the devil. Sadly, placing curses on people has become popular. One can even find many books that will teach people how to curse or cast spells on others.

We cannot control what another person does when they choose to harm us through the assistance of the devil. However, what is in our control is to make sure we are safeguarding ourselves from these attacks by making ourselves spiritually strong. Curses are only effective when we are weak in our faith. They take advantage of our lack of commitment to God and try to bring about our ruin. I have dealt with many people who have told me they had been cursed and it was affecting their relationships, businesses, finances, and so on. What was common in most of them was that they were not living out their relationship with God. The curse entered the cracks in their spirituality and began the process of turning their lives into a massive jumble of bits and pieces filled with anxiety and despair. Once when I was speaking on a college campus in the Midwest, a young man with a crystal around his neck was trying to place a curse on me as I was giving my presentation. It amazes me that people believe the tools of the devil are more powerful than the works of God.

4. Being Dedicated to a Demon through Satanic Ritual Abuse

Someone under the age of reason cannot bring evil upon themselves. The Church teaches that seven is the age of reason because when a child reaches this age, they have a good understanding of right and wrong. That is why a child usually makes their first confession when they are seven. If someone under the age of reason is experiencing extraordinary demonic activity in their lives, then someone who has authority over them, such as a parent or guardian, would bear the culpability for what the child is experiencing.

One of the exorcisms that I was able to observe while training in Rome was a young lady who shared with me that her mother had dedicated her to Satan when she was born. The mother did not want the child and blamed God for giving her a child she did not want. To get even with God, the mother decided to dedicate the child to Satan. For the first twelve years of her life, she went through all kinds of satanic rituals and abuses until she was able to run away from home. Living on the streets for over five years and facing all kinds of hardship, she finally turned to the Church for help. Through the prayers of the Church, she was set free from her demonic possession.

What we must learn from this example is that no one who is experiencing evil, especially one who has been dedicated to a demon, is ever lost completely to God. A demon cannot dominate a person in all their faculties. The intellect and free will of the person always remain free. "These are sacred spaces that no creature may enter. They are reserved for God alone who is the creator."[9] It is this part that remains free that can ask for the help of the Church.[10] This is extremely important because one may not have an exorcism prayed over them without their consent.

5. Abuse

Abuse can be an entry point for the demonic into a person's life because it can create emotional wounds that may cause a

---

[9] Bonino, *Angels and Demons*, 287.

[10] Amorth, *An Exorcist Explains the Demonic*, 66. "It is necessary to clarify that the devil is not able to take possession of one's soul (unless the person expressly consents to it), but only their body."

person to seek help from the wrong sources. While victims of abuse will not necessarily fall prey to demonic influence, through no fault of their own, a victim can become particularly vulnerable. Instead of turning to God, they may turn to those who say they can bring about the desired healing, such as witches or wizards. Evil cannot fix that which is broken. It will only break the person even more. Sadly, abuse is all too common in our society and as we know has even been committed by some of the clergy.

I once worked with a person who shared with me that she was repeatedly raped over a five-year period by a family member starting when she was seven years old. Broken and feeling unworthy of God's love, she turned to a witch who promised to make her whole. All she found was more brokenness and despair. With tears in her eyes, she asked if I could help her. When I responded that Jesus was going to help her, her eyes immediately turned green, her pupils became slanted like a serpent, and a demon manifested saying, "Who's he? He has no power over us." When I began to pray over her, the demon laughed at me and said, "You can't get rid of us. We've been here too long and you're not strong enough." When the official exorcism was performed a week later, after I breathed on the face of the person to call upon the Holy Spirit, the demon came out with a shriek and the person boldly proclaimed her freedom from the demonic and why she was worthy in the eyes of God. Exorcism prayers in these types of cases are powerful as they bring Christ into the brokenness caused by abuse. The healing one receives through these prayers makes the person whole and complete leaving no cracks for the devil to get a foothold.

6. LIFE OF HABITUAL SIN

There is a loss of the sense of sin in society today. Earlier I said that people are living by three guiding principles: (1) You may do as you wish, (2) No one has the right to command you, and (3) You are the god of yourself. When the serpent tempted Eve in the garden, we are told she "saw that the tree was good for food, and that it was a delight to the eyes" (Gen 3:6). Ever since that first sin against God's commands, humans have struggled with sin and have found delight in the things the devil has presented to us such as alcohol, drugs, pornography, and promiscuity. Rather than owning up to this sinful behavior, we constantly try to justify it by eliminating God from the picture. We no longer want to hear "The kingdom of God is at hand; repent, and believe in the gospel" (Mark 1:15). We want to believe only what we declare to be true and do not think we have anything from which to repent. The result is a life of habitual sin. This is something that delights the devil. Because the devil has placed many hidden traps along the way to the tree of life, Sacred Scripture teaches us to be on guard: "Know that you are walking in the midst of snares" (Sir 9:13) and "Take heed lest there be a base thought in your heart" (Deut 15:9).

The loss of the sense of sin has led to a rise in the number of requests for exorcism. Exorcists must respond since we are outposts for God's mercy. To those trapped in a life of habitual sin, we say return to the Lord through the Sacrament of Penance. Owning up to our sins opens us up to God's love and mercy. I once was contacted by a father who was concerned about his son's addiction to pornography. When I went to visit the young man, he refused to speak with me and there was a demonic manifestation whereby the evil spirit cursed and insulted the father and then slammed the door in our faces. I went into another room to speak with the father about the details surrounding his son, and as we were talking a deep voice shouted at us from another room, "Get out!" When I knocked on the door where the son was, the door immediately opened and the manifesting demon looked at me and in a child's voice said, "Hello, Fr. Vince." I demanded to speak with the young man, but the demon went screaming out the door. The son refused any assistance from me, so I was not able to help him.

7. Inviting a Demon into Your Life

It seems unimaginable that someone would deliberately invite a demon into their life. Yet it is a reality and a choice that people make for all sorts of reasons. A young man once told me that after he invited the demonic into his life and declared Satan to be his father, he encountered a power that exhilarated him and made him feel invincible. In sharing his story, he began to manifest by growling and hissing and his eyes rolled back into his head. He was referred to me by concerned family members. He rejected any help from the Church because he said his relationship with the devil is one that he did not want to end. He said the power he felt from Satan was so addictive there was no way he would be able to let go of it. There is also the story of an elderly man who fostered relationships with demons throughout his life. His family feared for his salvation since he had never accepted Christ. He told me it was his desire to spend eternity with the demons he had come to know and befriended in this life.

On another occasion a lady said she believed one of her friends was possessed, and in a misguided act of charity looked her friend in the face and said, "Whatever is in you I freely invite to come into me." No sooner did the words come out of her mouth than she felt a presence overtake her. She did want the help of the Church, and during the exorcism seven demons identified themselves in her. Leviathan was the dominant demon and the last of the seven to be cast out. It is a creature mentioned in the following biblical accounts: the Book of Job (3:8; 41:1), the Psalms (74:14; 104:26) and the Prophet Isaiah (27:1). When this demon manifested, it told me that it did not have to leave since it had been freely invited in. It is true that a person can use their free will to invite a demon into their life, and it is also true, contrary to what the demon might say, for them to use their free will to renounce the connection that was established. Therefore, using the Rite of Exorcism, I commanded Leviathan to leave since the person was now rejecting its presence. Ordering the demon to say "Hail Mary, full of grace" (Luke 1:28) and to depart immediately, the demon laughed, mocked me and said "grace of full." Commanding it to obey me in all things, although an unworthy minister of Christ, and to say the words in the proper order, and then to depart, the demon who had been speaking in a deep authoritative voice looked at me and in a child's voice said, "Hail Mary, full of grace." There was a scream and the demon departed. The lady sat in front of me beaming with the glory of God. This particular case lasted over a year. Someone asked me what I did to celebrate Christ's triumph over these seven demons, and I told them I went to Dairy Queen for a chocolate shake! The place was crowded and as I waited in line to place my order, I thought to myself that if these people knew where I had just come from I would be like Moses parting the Red Sea.

8. Unhealed Broken Relationships

The Church teaches that the family is the main building

block of society and as the family goes, so goes society. Families today are broken in so many ways, some reasons being divorce, political polarization, and those who have allowed their differences to reach such a level that they have not spoken to a parent or sibling for quite some time. Brokenness is a reality in all of our lives, and how we deal with it matters. Although broken relationships cannot always be repaired in this life, because of the unwillingness or inability of others, we can still seek our own healing. We can work to forgive others in our hearts, even if there is no possibility of face-to-face reconciliation. The devil loves it when we are at odds with each other. When we experience animosity, bitterness, resentment, anger, and revenge we can allow it to keep its grip on us, or we can choose to imitate the love and forgiveness of our Savior.

In Chapter 5 of Mark's Gospel, we hear the story of the Gerasene Demoniac. In this familiar biblical account, a man possessed by Legion is living in the tombs and chains will not hold him. Jesus rebukes the unclean spirits. They enter into the swine, rush down a steep bank, and drown in the sea. This is the end of the story as most people know it. But something particularly important happens once the exorcism has taken place. The man who is now free wants to go with Jesus, but Jesus refuses. Rarely in Sacred Scripture does Jesus tell someone not to follow him. This is a profound teaching moment. Instead of coming with him, Jesus tells the man to go home. A man who was living amongst the dead in the tombs is now placed amongst the living. In the world of exorcism, it is the unhealed broken relationships that the man experienced in his home that brought about the demonic possession. The lesson for us is that when we experience brokenness in our own homes, we can choose to make things bitter or we can choose to make them better. Bitter belongs to the devil. Better belongs to God. The devil fears people who love. "God is love" (1 John 4:8). When brokenness knocks at your door, always make the choice for God—when you do so, you put out the unwelcome mat for the devil.

AMERICAN PROTOCOL AND A DIOCESAN PROTOCOL

Where it is determined that the ministry of an exorcist is required, the decision to proceed with a major exorcism is made *only* after following strict protocols. The exorcist, in many ways, is trained to be a skeptic. I should be the last one to believe that someone is possessed. I must exhaust all reasonable explanations for what is taking place in the person. Therefore, experts in the medical and psychiatric sciences are always consulted.

People are often surprised to know that I utilize the services of mental health experts. Most people assume that it is the exorcist who sees possession and pulls out the Rite of Exorcism, whereas the psychiatrist sees mental illness and pulls out the DSM-5 or the medical doctor sees an illness and calls for tests. The truth is that psychology, medical science, and religion need not be at odds with each other. After all, the overriding goal should be to bring relief to the person who is suffering, whether that be due to mental, physical, or spiritual causes. The greatest debate surrounding the practice of exorcism is that there may be scientific explanations for behavior the Church considers to be evidence of diabolical possession.

Several psychological disorders, including Tourette syndrome and schizophrenia, can produce the types of effects seen in possessed people. People with epilepsy can suddenly go into convulsions when having a seizure; Tourette syndrome causes involuntary movements and vocal outbursts; schizophrenia involves auditory and visual hallucinations, paranoia, delusions, and sometimes violent behavior. Psychological issues like low self-esteem and narcissism can cause a person to act out the role of possessed person in order to gain attention. It is my opinion that in a case where the subject is in fact suffering from mental illness, the Church is doing greater harm by labeling the person possessed if this prevents the person from seeking out the medical or psychological treatment they require.

When the New Rite for Exorcism was released in 1999, Cardinal Jorge Medina Estevez, the Prefect for the Congregation for Divine Worship and the Discipline of the Sacraments, said, "exorcists must distinguish between the truly possessed and those who are suffering from hysteria or mental illness."[1] The challenge that many exorcists face is to find

---

[1] Excerpts of a press conference given by Cardinal Jorge Medina Estevez on January 26, 1999. *L'Osservatore Romano*, February 3, 1999.

a mental health expert who is at least open to the possibility that what the person is suffering from is some extraordinary activity of the devil. The truth is that not all would accept a spiritual cause for what is happening to the person. With that said, to help the exorcist to arrive at the point where he believes beyond a doubt that the person in front of him is possessed, there are certain protocols to be followed. One is adopted for use in the United States, and the other is one that has been adopted for use in the Archdiocese of Indianapolis.

The American Protocol

Each country needs to set up its own protocol based on whether or not the culture readily accepts the belief in the existence of God and angels and demons. Realistically, what might apply in one country may not apply in another. I saw this firsthand during a pastoral trip to South Africa in 2017. In a country where spiritual realities are culturally accepted, there was not a high emphasis placed on the need for a psychological evaluation before performing an exorcism. This contrasts with the United States where such realities are often called into question or outright rejected. With that said, here in the United States the following protocols have been put into place before a major exorcism may be performed:

+ A thorough physical examination by a qualified medical doctor with appropriate specialists consulted as needed.

+ A thorough psychological examination by a qualified clinical psychologist or psychiatrist, identifying all areas of concern. It is important to note that the Church is not asking these experts if they believe the person in question is possessed. The exorcist himself will make the final determination factoring in these expert opinions.

+ A "life history" of the person identifying where the entry point of evil may have originated, utilizing an Intake Questionnaire (included on the following pages).

+ Normalize the spiritual and sacramental life of the one who is possessed (energumen). It is not enough to simply cast the demon out, one also must invite God in. In the Gospel of Luke we are told, "When the unclean spirit has gone out of a man, he passes through the waterless places seeking rest; and finding none he says, 'I will return to my house from which I came.' And when he comes he finds it swept and put in order. Then he goes and brings seven other spirits more evil than himself, and they enter and dwell there; and the last state of that man becomes worse than the first" (11:24–26). Exorcism is always a matter of faith. No amount of exorcism can replace the central need in a person's life to accept the Lordship of Jesus Christ and to live out that relationship in an intimate, personal, and communal way.

+ Looking for the four extraordinary signs of demonic possession from the Rite of Exorcism. These include speaking languages otherwise unknown to the individual, exhibiting superhuman strength, knowledge of hidden things, and an aversion to anything of a sacred nature.

+ Careful compliance with diocesan legal and canonical processes. The exorcist must follow the norms of Canon Law and the diocesan norms put in place by his bishop.

+ The case is compiled and sent to the bishop requesting his permission for a major exorcism to take place in the diocese. The governing spirit rests with the local bishop, and he will make the final decision as to whether or not a major exorcism should be performed.

THE DIOCESAN PROTOCOL

+ Prior to referring the afflicted person to the diocesan exorcist, the pastor should meet the person to determine if something extraordinary or preternatural is occurring. Counseling may be helpful and advisable to rule out psychological reasons for the affliction. Likewise, a medical physical examination should be considered to rule out a fundamental medical condition as the cause. An Intake Questionnaire is included as a tool that may be used.

+ The pastor is expected to assist the individual to return to a life of faith or come to faith for the first time. Making a profound confession with the aid of the parish priest, encouraging regular Mass attendance, and beginning a strong prayer life are essential. A life of faith and commitment to Jesus Christ will resolve most demonic attacks. Without these initial steps, the efficacy of the diocesan exorcist will be extremely limited.

+ If deemed necessary, the pastor should contact the exorcist providing him with detailed information on the case from the Intake Questionnaire. The afflicted person should never be told to contact the exorcist directly. In cases of mental illness, this can deepen the distress of the person who may cling to a referral as confirmation of extraordinary demonic activity in their life.

+ The pastor will need to remain in contact with the afflicted person to provide on-going pastoral care.

+ The parish priest should be the first line of contact. Please do not delegate referrals to parish administrative staff; the exorcist needs to hear firsthand why this is believed to be a case of extraordinary demonic activity.

+ Do not provide the person seeking assistance with the

exorcist's telephone number or location. The exorcist will determine if he will see the individual or if he has recommendations for the pastor on how to follow up with the afflicted person. Redirecting an individual can lead to the assumption that their self-diagnosis is correct, and the exorcist is now obligated to resolve their issues.

+ The diocesan exorcist is always available to assist pastors in providing guidance on how to deal with those who believe they are possessed, as this is a situation for which many priests are not prepared.

+ Individuals outside of the local diocese must be directed to their local parish. The exorcist has no authority apart from his bishop. Each diocese will determine its own protocols when it comes to investigating alleged cases of extraordinary demonic activity. The Office of Exorcist in one diocese does collaborate and provide guidance to other dioceses.

Intake Questionnaire

The following questions (with some explanatory commentary) are suggested possibilities when approached by someone who believes they are suffering from extraordinary demonic activity:

+ *A person is asked to share their basic background, including marital status, age, religion, and so on.*

+ *Please describe the experience or experiences which lead you to believe that you are being affected by the presence of evil. What has been the frequency and duration of time that these experiences have occurred?*

> What I am looking for is what the person believes to be the entry point for the evil in their life. I am also interested in what types of manifestations the person might be experiencing. This allows me to have a better understanding of the number of possible demons and the extent of their power.

+ *Is there an event or series of events which create the impression of evil?*

> In other words, does something trigger the manifestation of evil? For example, did the person go on a haunted tour, watch a scary movie, or participate in a ghost hunt or visit to a cemetery?

+ *Please describe your psychological history: Have there been any periods of psychotherapy and if so, about what issues? Are you currently under the care of a psychiatrist or any other type of therapist? Are you currently taking any medication prescribed by a doctor? If so, what kind and type? Have you discussed these occurrences with a thera-*

pist? (*The priest may want to ask for permission from the individual to speak with the therapist*).

The purpose of this question is to understand if the person has been diagnosed with any type of mental health issue and if they are currently being treated for it by a psychiatrist or psychologist. I want to be incredibly careful not to say something at an initial interview whereby I discount all the work that has been done through the mental health profession.

+ *Have you had any history with chemical addiction or abuse with drugs or alcohol?*

Habitual sin in the form of alcohol and drug abuse can be an entry point for evil, but one also must see their own personal responsibility in overcoming these addictions. It is too easy to lay the blame for all our struggles on the devil. We still must exercise personal responsibility, and if the devil is trying to use these addictions to enter into our lives, then we are not completely powerless to turn to Christ for healing.

+ *Have you had any history with the use of pornography through the media, internet, magazines, television, et cetera? What kind of music do you listen to? Frequency?*

What kind of movies and / or television programs do you watch? Frequency?

Pornography is a major scourge on humanity right now as it reduces the human person to a mere object for another's pleasure. It is sickening that children are being exposed to it at such an early age. The devil uses pornography to disfigure the human person who has been created in the image and likeness of God. The devil believes that he is getting even with God by attacking God's greatest creation. The danger of certain types of music is that it glorifies evil and is subliminally putting demonic thoughts and ideas in our minds.

+ *Have you had any experience or history of engaging in the occult: witchcraft, magic, magicians, fortune tellers, crystals, wizards, or game boards that are linked to the occult?*

It is important to know if people have turned to the occult and if they believe in its power. Have they surrendered either knowingly or unknowingly to the power and forces of evil?

+ *Have you had any relationships or contact with people who are associated with the occult or satanic practices?*

The people we spend time with can influence our thoughts and beliefs. If we are spending time with people involved in the occult, then these relationships can have an adverse effect on us.

+ *Have you ever attended a satanic black mass or other satanic ritual? Have you ever tried to communicate with spirits, demons, or the devil itself?*

    It is important to know if anyone has attempted direct contact with the devil or any other evil spirits. They seek relationships with us in order to destroy us by having our lives unravel when we try to engage with them. We cannot use the devil, but he will always use us. We might think we have the upper hand and the devil is in our control, but the only person we are fooling is ourselves.

+ *To the best of your knowledge, has anyone ever placed a curse on you?*

    This question allows me to know the extent of the person's level of faith. Curses are only effective when we are weak in our commitment to Jesus Christ. We cannot control someone who wishes to be engaged in the world of curses, spells, and hexes, but we can control ourselves and make sure that we are surrounding ourselves with God's grace. This is more powerful than any demonic curse that someone might want to send our way.

- *Do you have any aversion to sacred objects or rituals that have become part of your personal experience?*

  One sign of demonic possession is the aversion to anything of a sacred nature. This includes things like a Bible, crucifix, rosary, relic, or holy water. To rule out someone trying to feign possession, the exorcist may bless the person with unblessed water to see what type of reaction it creates. The exorcist and the demon will know if the water has been blessed, but the person will not.

- *Has anything strange ever occurred in your life for which you have no logical explanation?*

  This question allows the person to examine their life and share with the exorcist anything else that may have occurred in their life that is outside of the ordinary. For example, has the person had a vision, particular dream, or been visited by a spirit?

- *Have you read any books or done any research on the topic of exorcism?*

  The exorcist wants to determine that the fascination with the topic of exorcism has not led the person to self-diagnose and convince themselves they are possessed. It is much like the person who picks up a medical journal and then begins to believe they have the symptoms of some particular illness.

+ *Have you been "prayed over" or "exorcized" by an individual or group? Have you turned to someone else for help before seeking help from the Church?*

There are many deliverance groups that provide a great ministry to those who are afflicted by evil. It is also true that the devil may try to infiltrate these groups so that when a person turns to them for help, they are ultimately left in a worse condition than before. People should never let someone pray over them before they know something about them because people are not always what they seem to be.

+ *How would you describe your own personal self-discipline? How do you deal with personal limits?*

This question gives the exorcist insight into a person's state of mind. Do they think they are free to do whatever they want, or do they recognize that limitations are a form of obedience that allow us to grow in holiness and virtue? Does the person understand that just because the human person is capable of something does not mean that it is the right thing to do?

+ *What avenues of healing have you already sought?*
    + *Spiritual*
    + *Medical (including any therapy and medication)*
    + *Counseling*

    It is important to understand how the person has tried to fix their brokenness before turning to an exorcist.

+ *Has anyone involved in the occult ever given you anything that is still in your possession?*

    This question investigates if demonic infestation may be at play through some object that has been placed on their person or property. This might include a cursed object or one that has gone through some type of satanic ritual. Some examples would be a voodoo doll or a locket of one's hair.

+ *Do you truly want to be free of the evil influences you believe are presently affecting you? Will you do what must be done?*

    Just because someone is asking for help does not mean they are willing to do what needs to be done to break the connection with evil. The person must be willing to follow the direction of the exorcist. When I take on a case, I require the person to work directly with me and no other exorcist. In my experience, people who believe they are possessed will have called or contacted several other exorcists. Too many cooks spoil the broth, so to speak, and the person must be willing to follow my direction and not continue to consult with other exorcists.

This Intake Questionnaire is an invaluable tool in the hands of the exorcist as it allows him to better understand the person seeking help and what they are experiencing. Due to the volume of people who seek my help, this questionnaire is provided to all the parish priests in my diocese, who are asked to complete it with the person in their area who is seeking help. Once it is completed, then it is forwarded on to me. The great thing about this tool is that it gives the parish priest a starting point on how to respond and minister to those who believe they are dealing with extraordinary demonic activity.

To all those who believe they are being afflicted by the evil one, I would offer the following advice. Do not go to your local priest and tell him you are possessed. That scenario is not addressed in most seminary formation programs. Your diagnosis will leave him not knowing how to help you, and you will only find yourself more frustrated. It is better for you to go to him and say there is something going on in your life that you cannot explain, and you need his spiritual guidance and direction. By listening to you, he can then direct you to the exorcist in your diocese who can provide you with more direct pastoral care.

The Ordinary Activity
of the Devil

Very few of us will ever have to be concerned about demonic infestation, vexation, obsession, and possession. Heads spinning, pea soup flying, bodies levitating, and someone crawling up a wall like a spider certainly gets lots of attention. The truth is that while much has been said about the extraordinary activity of the devil, very little has been said about the ordinary activity of the devil. "The devil is far less to be feared in so-called manifestations than in the underground influence he exerts in souls that are not sufficiently instructed or well-tempered."[1] In other words, we need to be more aware of how the devil attacks all of us in the ordinary circumstances of our daily lives in a very quiet and subtle way.

The devil's ultimate goal is to fracture our prayer life, faith life, moral life, sacramental life, and our relationships

---

[1] Jean Lhermitte, *True or False Possession? How to Distinguish the Demonic from the Demented* (Manchester, NH: Sophia Institute Press, 2013), 18.

with one another in such a way that we are pulled further and further away from God. And the further we are removed from God, the more we lose our sense of identity. When we are connected with God, we know what it means to be human. When we are disconnected from God, the image of the human person becomes distorted. The devil uses his ordinary activity to disconnect us from God whereby we become more isolated, turned in on ourselves, and more susceptible to believing the lies that the devil is presenting. In his ordinary demonic activity, the devil wants his lies to become the truth in the mind of the human person. He did this with Adam and Eve in the Garden of Eden, and he continues this same plan of attack today. All of us need to better understand how the devil tries to ruin us by pulling us away from God in the ordinary circumstances of our lives.

The human person seeks intimacy with God. This is best reflected in the writings of St. Augustine: "Great are You, O Lord, and greatly to be praised; great is Your power, and of Your wisdom there is no end. And man, being part of Your creation, desires to praise You—man, who bears about with him his mortality, the witness of his sin, even the witness that You 'resist the proud,'—yet man, this part of Your creation, desires to praise You. You move us to delight in praising You; for You have made us for Yourself, and our hearts are restless until they rest in You."[2] The devil wants to destroy this

---

[2] Augustine, *Confessions*, Book 1.

intimacy with God by intruding into our daily lives in very harmful ways. He wants to get us to sin because "every sin strengthens Satan's hold on this world"[3] and gets us off the path that is leading to the tree of life.

Fr. Louis J. Cameli has written a book that has deeply influenced my understanding of the ordinary activity of the devil.[4] He was one of my teachers when I attended the University of St. Mary of the Lake in Mundelein, Illinois. He says that the devil uses a four-stage plan of attack on us. It begins with deception, that leads to division, that leads to diversion, and ends in discouragement. Each of these four stages of ordinary demonic activity is worth exploring.

The devil uses deception to create doubt and confusion when it comes to the truth as revealed by God. He wants to turn things inside out, upside down, and to invert reality so that we begin to perceive his lies as truth. He did this with Eve and the fruit of the tree in the middle of the garden when he said to her, "'You will not die. For God knows that when you eat of it your eyes will be opened, and you will be like God, knowing good and evil.' So when the woman saw that the tree was good for food, and it was a delight to the eyes, and that the tree was to be desired to make one wise, she took of its fruit and ate; and she also gave some to her husband,

---

[3] Suenens, *Renewal and the Powers of Darkness*, 41.
[4] Louis J. Cameli, *The Devil You Don't Know: Recognizing and Resisting Evil in Everyday Life* (Notre Dame, IN: Ave Maria Press, 2011).

and he ate." (Gen 3:4b–5). What the devil was successful in doing was to convince Adam and Eve that good and evil no longer depended on God but on one's own interpretations. He used deception to convince the human person to act independently of the law of God. We all need to realize this is what the devil tries to do with us. "Deception is embedded in everyday life to try and pull us away from God. [The devil] has no need for dramatic effects. He moves subtly and stealthily so that he draws us into a deceived way of seeing, understanding, and acting, but he does so in a deceitful way that seems entirely unremarkable and often unnoticeable."[5]

The result of this deception is that the human person becomes the law and measure of all things. "Once God's authority is called into question, everything will collapse. People will go so far as to ask: 'Who is God to impose that on me?' In rejecting God's authority, they will end up rejecting the cogency of the divine law and, finally, they will call into question the goodness and relevance of God's commandments. They will then turn to the law of men or, more precisely, to the law of the strongest."[6] The devil fell from heaven because he wanted to have the final say in how things should be. He was disobedient to God's plan, and now he had convinced humanity to follow the same path. And as with him, things

---

5 Cameli, *The Devil You Don't Know*, 55.
6 Jean-Charles Nault, OSB, *The Noonday Devil: Acedia, the Unnamed Evil of Our Times* (San Francisco, CA: Ignatius Press, 2013), 100.

would only get worse. By buying into the devil's lies, we are led to the second plan of attack the devil uses in his ordinary activity to trip us up; namely, division.

Once we have bought into the lies of the devil, we should not be surprised that he now wants to sow division. He desires to divide people from God, from each other, and from their very selves.[7] After Adam and Eve sinned, they went and hid from God, not together but apart. Rather than owning up to their actions, they kept pointing the blame. When God asked Adam what he had done, he pointed to Eve. When God asked Eve what she had done, she pointed to the serpent. They had now chosen a world of ugliness and lies over the world of the beauty and truth that God had given them.

God wants a sense of cohesion and unity in his creation. The devil just wants a bunch of broken pieces. He can make us feel overwhelmed as though something is out of our reach, beyond our capacity, so that we will give up. He also stirs up our fear to make us feel frightened so that we will withdraw or not live up to our potential. He can suggest that we compare ourselves to others, usually to the extent that we overestimate the abilities of others and underestimate our own, so that we look bad in comparison. He sets us up against each other with the likes of anger, resentment, contempt, greed, and avarice. He can stir up impatience, so that we become agitated and dissatisfied. He can short-circuit our journey with

7   Cameli, *The Devil You Don't Know*, 57.

drugs and various forms of addictions or infidelity.[8] Some examples are the opioid crisis, alcohol abuse, addiction to pornography, the breakup of the family through divorce, and the attack on the unborn through abortion. This brokenness leads us to the third plan of attack that the devil uses in his ordinary activity; namely, diversion.

Once the devil has gotten us to buy into his lies and has divided us into a mass of broken pieces, his next plan of attack is diversion. The devil desires that we divert ourselves from the pathway of God. God has a plan for everyone, and this is something the devil does not want us to discover. His goal in diversion is to have us lose our focus and our sense of purpose and direction whereby we believe we can act independently of God. The devil tried this with Jesus when he tempted him in the desert, and he tries it with us as well. In the world of diversion, we replace God with ourselves and operate under three guiding principles that I mentioned earlier: You may do as you wish, no one has the right to command you, and you are the god of yourself. Diversion acts in a subtle way. Often, we do not realize that we are off course and perhaps have been off course for a while.[9]

All of us are on a journey to the tree of life. With diversion, the devil wants us to believe that we are not on a journey and that this world is our final destination. The devil tells us

8   Cameli, *The Devil You Don't Know*, 59–60.
9   Cameli, *The Devil You Don't Know*, 92.

that we do not need God because paradise is something we create here and now according to our own truths. Buying into this line of thinking is extremely dangerous because "if there is no stable truth, no grounding, then there is no specific direction that is right or appropriate."[10] The end result is relativism, something that Pope Benedict XVI spoke of often.

What we need to realize is that when our eyes are diverted from God, there is no utopia. Rather, society becomes a free-for-all and is marked by the likes of anger, fear, anxiety, addiction, abuse, violence, hatred, instant gratification, and treating others as disposable objects. Without God in the picture, the end product is a world of busyness and distraction whereby we always have to be doing something or engaged in some meaningless activity. It is a world of noise that drowns out the voice of God, and the only voice we hear is ourselves. Archbishop Daniel Buechlein was fond of saying that the Church has all the vocations that it needs, but young people cannot hear God calling them to the priesthood and religious life because his voice is drowned out by the distractions and lure of the things of this world. Just consider for a moment how we have replaced God with technology and all our gadgets. Technology and its tools have their place, but things of our own creation cannot become a substitute for the uncreated God.

Everything we do in this life should be leading us closer to God and not further away from him. It is important for us

---

[10] Cameli, *The Devil You Don't Know*, 114.

to remember that when God created us, he made us *human beings*, not *human doings*. Our value comes not from what we do, but simply from the fact that we are. By trapping us in a world of busyness whereby we are absorbed in all the tasks at hand, the devil diverts us from God and causes us to lose our sense of identity. When we no longer know who we truly are—a reflection of the divine image—discouragement sets in.

After the devil has led us down the pathway of deception, to division, to diversion, finally we arrive at discouragement. In the Christian tradition, discouragement is referred to as acedia. It is a word first used by the Christian monk and ascetic, Evagrius of Pontus (AD 346–399). Living in the Egyptian desert, he wrote about his experiences in combatting evil spirits, in particular, the demon of acedia, which he called the noonday devil. It is a reference to Psalm 91 [90]:6 where we are told that we need not fear "the destruction that lays waste at noonday."

Acedia is the final stage of the devil's ordinary activity, and it is the most dangerous threat to the spiritual life and our journey to God. Acedia is the lack of joy and tiredness that shows itself on the faces of far too many people. These are the people we see in the car next to us at a stoplight, walking a city street, standing in line in front of us at the checkout, or, sitting with a long face in the pew with us at weekend Mass. Acedia speaks of depression and "depression's neighbor is despair—the utter forsaking of all hope."[11] Hope is the key ingredient to the Christian life. It lets us know that whatever we are dealing with, whatever we are experiencing, wherever we find ourselves is not the end of the story; there is more to come. Hope is exemplified in Jesus on the Cross. His death marks not the end but a new beginning.

The devil wants to take Jesus' gift of hope away from us. His main weapon is acedia. Evagrius says that acedia is the "relaxation of the soul,"[12] or "a lack of spiritual energy."[13] Just consider the great number of people who have grown up in Christian homes who have now left the Church saying that God does not exist or is no longer relevant. These newly professed atheists reject anything that has to do with God, especially the Church, and only embrace science. The Church is viewed as out of step with the modern world, whereas science can provide us with all the answers we need. The danger is that "a society affected by acedia ends up affirming that the sciences must be able to explain everything, prove everything; moreover, it thinks it is legitimate—or even necessary, to implement and experience all that science is capable of achieving."[14] Acedia causes us to act without limits and this is demonstrated in the likes of cloning, abortion, and euthanasia. This deification of the human person

---

[11] Cameli, *The Devil You Don't Know*, 126.
[12] Evagrius of Pontus, *On the Eight Thoughts* 13, *in Greek Ascetic Corpus*, 83.
[13] Nault, *The Noonday Devil*, 28.
[14] Nault, *The Noonday Devil*, 184.

has caused us to act without limits. Just because humanity is capable of something does not mean it is permissible in the eyes of God.

When people have journeyed through the stages of the ordinary activity of the devil and arrive at acedia and the discouragement, emptiness, exhaustion, dejection, restlessness, and monotony that comes with it, I believe we have arrived at a crossroads. We can resign ourselves to the fact that we are walking the pathway of the devil or we can choose the pathway of Jesus Christ. The devil promises death. Jesus Christ promises life. In John's Gospel, he tells us, "I came that they may have life, and have it abundantly" (10:10). When faced with acedia, we must recommit ourselves to Jesus Christ. He says to all of us, "I am the way, and the truth, and the life; no one comes to the Father, but by me" (John 14:6). I believe when we rediscover Jesus' rightful place in our lives, that is the call of the New Evangelization of which St. John Paul II spoke.[15]

The main tool used to bring people back to Jesus Christ and out of the clutches of the devil is the Word of God. Evagrius believed that Sacred Scripture has the power to defeat acedia. He writes, "In the time of struggle, when demons make war against us and hurl their arrows at us [cf. Eph

---

[15] Pope St. John Paul II, Apostolic Letter on the Permanent Validity of the Church's Missionary Mandate *Redemptoris Missio* (December 7, 1990).

6:16], let us answer them from the Holy Scriptures."[16] He was influenced by such great figures as St. Athanasius (AD 296–373) and St. Anthony of the Desert (AD 251–356). St. Athanasius says that passages from the Bible send demons away in terror because "the Lord is in the words of the Scriptures."[17] St. Anthony used "biblical verses, especially from the Psalms [as] his most favorite spiritual weapons."[18] "By consciously using good thoughts drawn from the Bible to cut off bad ones suggested by the demons,"[19] we have the power to overcome the ordinary attacks of the devil. The best example of the power of the Word of God in defeating the devil is found in Matthew's Gospel:

> Then Jesus was led up by the Spirit into the wilderness to be tempted by the devil. And he fasted forty days and forty nights, and afterward he was hungry. And the tempter came and said to him, "If you are the Son of God, command these stones to become loaves of bread." But he answered, "It is written, 'Man shall not live by bread alone, but by every word that proceeds from the mouth of God.'" Then the devil took him to the holy city, and set him on the pinnacle

---

[16] Evagrius of Pontus, *Talking Back: A Monastic Handbook for Combating Demons*, trans. David Brakke (Collegeville, MN: Liturgical Press, 2009), 49.

[17] Athanasius, *Epistle to Marcellinus*, 33.

[18] Evagrius of Pontus, *Talking Back*, 20.

[19] Evagrius of Pontus, *Talking Back*, 28.

of the temple, and said to him, "If you are the Son of God, throw yourself down; for it is written, 'He will give his angels charge of you,' and 'On their hands they will bear you up, lest you strike your foot against a stone.'" Jesus said to him, "Again it is written, 'You shall not tempt the Lord your God.'" Again, the devil took him to a very high mountain, and showed him all the kingdoms of the world and the glory of them; and he said to him, "All these I will give you, if you fall down and worship me." Then Jesus said to him, "Begone, Satan! for it is written, 'You shall worship the Lord your God and him alone shall you serve.'" Then the devil left him, and behold, angels came and ministered to him. (4:1–11)

The important lesson that we learn from this passage is that the words of Sacred Scripture are an effective weapon against the temptations of the devil. It is worth noting that we cannot simply mouth the words of Scripture, for even the devil was able to do that. Rather, we must truly understand them and make them part of ourselves by speaking them from the heart.

A Word to Priests

If there was ever a time that the priesthood needed a clearer identity, that time is certainly now. The Church continues to struggle with the clergy sex abuse crisis, fewer ordinations, lower Mass attendance, weaker participation in the sacramental life of the Church, and an exodus of so many young people from her pews. The devil knows those who are working to defeat him and will use many avenues to try to destroy the Church. Attacking the priesthood is one of his favorite weapons. The goal of a Christian is to reach the tree of life, and priests are the ones who Jesus has called to guide us to our ultimate destination. The devil believes that if the priesthood can be destroyed, then people will lose their way. One of the devil's favorite tactics is to get a priest to begin to see his priesthood as an occupation rather than a vocation. In some respects, his plan seems to be working. Many priests today find themselves juggling multiple parish assignments and simply going from one activity to the next. At times we may feel as if we are living in our cars. The danger here is that busyness can lead to fatigue, and fatigue can lead to frustration and viewing the people we are called to serve as a burden as opposed to the blessing they truly are. A vocation in the true sense of the word means a calling from God.

When I am asked why I chose to become a priest, I am always quick to respond that I chose this life because I believe it is what God wanted me to do. To serve God and his Church is one of the most rewarding and fulfilling vocations that one can receive. At the heart of priesthood must be service to the people of God. How we minister to people who believe they are up against the forces of evil is one of the avenues that can help the priesthood to rediscover its true identity.

On Holy Thursday in 2013, Pope Francis spoke on the topic of the priesthood. As he celebrated the Chrism Mass, at which he blessed the oils used in the various sacraments of the Church, he reminded all priests that we carry on our shoulders the people entrusted to our care. He wanted to address priestly identity and to suggest that if there is a crisis in the priesthood it is because priests have lost their focus on what it means to be called to the Sacrament of Holy Orders. The Holy Father wanted to remind all priests that we must be about service to the people of God and to avoid the temptation to get so caught up in the trappings of this world that we neglect the weightier matter of the glory of God resplendent in his people. He said we must be about *unction* and not *function*. We must see as our number one priority the anointing of people with the gladness of Jesus Christ. We do this by being priests who are filled with great hope and joy and who want to spread the Good News of Jesus Christ to a world that is burdened by so many things today that it robs them of the joy God wants them to have. This is an important message because there are so many people today, and for so many reasons, who have lost their spiritual footing and who need some help finding their way back to the path that leads to Jesus Christ. As priests, let us be those people who help others find their way.

The parish priest is on the frontlines of dealing with people who are up against the attacks of the evil one. Perhaps you might feel inadequate in dealing with these situations. People who are troubled can be relentless with their phone calls, leaving long messages begging for help, sending emails demanding responses, dropping into the parish unannounced and expecting immediate help, lurking after Mass to confront you at the most inopportune time. Simply brushing them off and trying to get them to leave or sending them elsewhere is not helpful. If a budget meeting or our favorite television program is more important than helping someone who comes to us asking for help because they believe they are being afflicted by the evil one, what does that say about our priorities? Priests share in the mission of Jesus Christ and his entire mission is directed towards freeing people from demonic influence. We read in the First Letter of John, "The reason the Son of God appeared was to destroy the works of the devil" (3:8). If this was Jesus' mission, then it now falls to us. I believe that helping those who are afflicted by evil reaffirms our priestly identity.

The things I would emphasize in the life of the priest are the following:

+ **Be a man with a renewed faith in Jesus Christ.** We are not freed or saved by a formula, or a doctrine but by a Person, and that Person's name is Jesus Christ. Make sure that we are truly living in a permanent connection with Jesus Christ. Jesus promised to be with us always and it is essential that he be at the center of our priesthood. Do not isolate yourselves in your rectories. Be in a support group. Go to diocesan gatherings. Go on retreat. Bless people and things. One of my former archbishops often reminded the priests in the archdiocese that it was possible to still live in the rectory while having internally left the priesthood. Let us all make the choice to be an outpost for God's mercy and not simply managers of our parishes. Showing people the face of God will help to re-evangelize the world.

+ **Be a man of integrity.** Victory over Satan and the pain and misery he inflicts on people depends on how much our souls remain pure from every worldly vice. Temptation is real for priests. It will be waged first in our spiritual and priestly life. In the face of the devil's attacks against us, Jesus reminds us in the Gospel of John (17:14), that like him, we must not be of this world. In other words, we must not allow ourselves to get caught up in the trappings that that this world has to offer, for in doing so we deflect ourselves from the work to which God has called us to be about. St. Paul reminds us that the best defense against the devil's attacks is to, "Put on the whole armor of God, that you may be able to stand against the wiles of the devil" (Eph 6:11). Satan will attack us as we fight against him. For this reason, the armor of God is so important. That armor is the power of the Holy Spirit. Because enveloped in the Holy Spirit, the priest can understand how to defeat the powers of evil and help those who have fallen under the power of the devil. Later in his Letter to the Ephesians St. Paul says, "Therefore take the whole armor of God, that you may be able to withstand in the evil day, and having done all, to stand. Stand therefore, having fastened the belt of truth around your waist, and having put on the breastplate of righteousness, and having shod your feet with the equipment of the gospel of peace; besides all these, taking the shield of faith, with which you can quench all the flaming darts of the Evil One. And take the helmet of salvation, and the sword of the Spirit, which is the word of God" (Eph 6:13–17).

+ **Be a man of prayer.** Prayer is a gift of grace that demands diligence and presupposes a commitment which can sometimes be wearisome. Prayer connects us to God and the devil will do all he can to turn us away from prayer and union with God. Do not let prayer become mechanical. Celebrate Mass reverently. Go to confession. Pray before the Blessed Sacrament. Read the Bible. Practice Marian devotion. Pray the rosary. Pray the Liturgy of the Hours.

+ **Be a man of humility.** Be willing to fast, suffer, and make sacrifice. The Servant of God Fr. Candido Amantini, who spent his life doing exorcisms at the Santa Scala in Rome, reminded those who trained under him that in order to fulfill the mission of exorcism one must cultivate prayer with a spirit of serious sacrifice. He fasted and often spent the night in prayer, depriving himself of rest and imposing on himself acts of penance and mortification. Although his advice was specifically directed to exorcists, his emphasis on prayer and fasting is an important lesson for all priests.

+ **Be a man who heals.** Lack of faith and the loss of the sense of sin have caused the devil to unleash many attacks against humanity. We must help people confront these attacks and rebuild their lives. The evil one hides in woundedness and isolation. There are a lot of broken people in the world. Let us help them put the pieces back together and not fracture them even more by not having time for the people who turn to us. We have the power to release people from their darkness because we have the key to the chains that bind. That key is Jesus Christ. Bless people. Get people to tell you where they are in the relationship with Christ. Ask them, "How are you and Jesus doing?" If they have been using an item from the occult, such as a Ouija Board or tarot cards, get them to give these things to you so you can dispose of them. Indeed, helping those who are afflicted by evil makes the Gospel come more fully alive as people begin to see its relevancy in their lives. It is no longer a theory, but something practical that can transform their brokenness into something whole and complete. Pope Francis, in a homily during Mass in Santa Marta on May 2, 2015, said, "Sometimes, I speak of the Church as if it were a field hospital. It's true: there are so many, many wounded! So many people who need their wounds healed! This is the mission of the Church."

All these things can be summed up by being a Man of God. This, I believe, is the most important, characteristic of the priesthood. I am reminded of the following biblical account when God says to Moses and Aaron to, "'Take your rod and cast it down before Pharaoh, that it may become a serpent.' So Moses and Aaron went to Pharaoh and did as the Lord commanded; Aaron cast down his rod before Pharaoh and his servants, and it became a serpent. Then Pharaoh summoned the wise men and the sorcerers; and they also, the magicians of Egypt, did the same by their secret arts. For every man cast down his rod, and they became serpents. But Aaron's rod swallowed up their rods" (Exod 7:9–12). What distinguishes the actions of Moses and Aaron from those of Pharaoh's magicians? Moses and Aaron were men of God. It was not what they were doing. It was the power of God working through them. As priests of Jesus Christ, we must be able to see the power of God at work in us. It is through the power of Jesus at work in us, by virtue of our priesthood, that people can be liberated from the evil that afflicts them.

Best Practices to Fend Off the Devil

Christians should not live in fear of the devil. We are called to be God-fearing people and what this means is that we live in awe of God and all that he is doing in our lives because of his great love for each of us. Our strength comes from "the Lord's Resurrection, in the triumph of life over death, of love over hatred, of truth over falsehood, of light over darkness."[1] Three hundred and sixty-five times throughout the Bible we are told in one form or another "Be Not Afraid." Literally, once for every day of the year, God reminds us that evil is something that we should not fear. One example comes to us from the Second Book of Kings:

> When the servant of the man of God rose early in the morning and went out, behold, an army with horses and chariots was round about the city. And the servant said, "Alas, my master! What shall we do?" He

---

[1] Suenens, *Renewal and the Powers of Darkness*, 105.

said, "Fear not, for those who are with us are more than those who are with them." Then Eli'sha prayed, and said, "O Lord, I beg you, open his eyes that he may see." So the Lord opened the eyes of the young man, and he saw; and behold the mountain was full of horses and chariots of fire round about Eli'sha. (6:15–17)

These verses remind us that although "it may seem like an uneven match—the human against the demon—but we have the assistance of divine grace and the angels."[2] We should always remember that the forces of good always outnumber the forces of evil. A great remark from St. Theresa of Avila, the sixteenth century Spanish mystic, says, "I don't understand those fears that make us cry, the devil, the devil, when we can say God, God!"[3]

Unclean spirits vary in strength, boldness, and malice. They can influence our thoughts by way of the imagination, and they can excite feelings in us, such as lust, anger, or despair. Using their Evening Knowledge, they can deduce what we might be thinking by watching us closely and noting the effects they are producing in us. They have their specialties, and in order to implant their particular vice, they look for the opportune time and place when we are weakest and let our guard down. Their power over us will either increase or

[2] Bonino, *Angels and Demons*, 298.
[3] Suenens, *Renewal and the Powers of Darkness*, 105.

decrease according to the level of resistance they meet in us. We make ourselves strong against the devil's attacks when we choose the love of God over the fear the devil is trying to sow.

In the First Letter of John we read, "Perfect love casts out fear" (4:18). Love deepens our faith and "what lies at the heart of our faith is not demonology, but Jesus Christ."[4] Our focus must always be on him and him alone, not on what demons are trying to do to us. Demons have no power over us except that which we surrender to them. They can propose but they cannot impose. The best defense against the forces of evil is for each of us to live out our faith and to grow in our relationship and commitment to Jesus Christ. I want to share with you some very concrete examples of what all of us can do to focus on Christ and in doing so, defeat the devil:

+ **Read and know the Bible.** St. Jerome (AD 347–420) said, "Ignorance of Scripture is ignorance of Christ." Therefore, to know Scripture is to know Christ and his power.

  Here are a few examples:

  > Besides this you know what hour it is, how it is full time now for you to wake from sleep. The night is far gone, the day is at hand. Let us cast off the works of darkness and put on

---

[4] Suenens, *Renewal and the Powers of Darkness*, 107.

the armor of light; let us conduct ourselves becomingly as in the day. But put on the Lord Jesus Christ. (Rom 13:11a, 12–13a, 14a)

Take the whole armor of God, that you may be able to withstand in the evil day, and having done all, to stand. (Eph 6:13)

I have been crucified with Christ; it is no longer I who live, but Christ who lives in me; and the life I now live in the flesh I live by faith in the Son of God, who loved me and gave himself for me. (Gal 2:20)

Submit yourselves therefore to God. Resist the devil and he will flee from you. Draw near to God and he will draw near to you. Cleanse your hands, you sinners, and purify your hearts, you men of double mind. Humble yourselves before the Lord and he will exalt you. (Jas 4:7–8, 10)

The Word of God is the most effective tool that we can use to defeat the devil. Jesus used it to renounce the temptations of the devil at the beginning of his public ministry, and in doing so, teaches us to do the same.

+ **Practice Marian Devotion.** The Blessed Mother is a powerful ally for anyone who is up against the forces of evil. The devil could not touch the Blessed Mother because she was full of grace. Fr. Gabriele Amorth recounts the story of a fellow exorcist who once asked the devil what are the qualities of the Most Holy Mother Mary that make you so angry and cause you so much pain? The devil responded that she is the purest of everyone, and he is the filthiest; she is the humblest, and he is the most rebellious; she is the most obedient, and he never obeys.[5] The Blessed Mother also teaches us that every hour is the hour for Christ. In the story of the Marriage at Cana, Jesus says to his mother, "My hour has not yet come" (John 2:4). Her response is, "Do whatever he tells you" (John 2:5). These are the final words she speaks in the Bible. Once she tells us to listen to and obey Jesus, she has said all that needs to be said.

+ **Frequent the Sacraments.** The devil is fought positively and preventively by everything that nourishes and strengthens the Christian life, and therefore, above all, by recourse to the sacraments.[6] As Catholics we need to go to confession and attend Holy Mass with the reception of Holy Communion. St. Ignatius of An-

---

[5] Amorth, *My Battle Against Satan*, 40.
[6] Suenens, *Renewal and the Powers of Darkness*, 17.

tioch (AD 35–108) stresses the importance of Holy Mass in his Letter to the Ephesians where he writes, "Do your best, then, to meet more often and to give thanks and glory to God. When you meet frequently, the powers of Satan are confounded, and in the face of your corporate faith his maleficence crumbles" (no. 13). Our Catholic faith must not be purely cultural, by which we merely go through the motions. It must be a lived relationship with Jesus Christ exemplified through the sacramental life of the Church.

+ **Pray and Fast.** When the disciples asked Jesus why they were not able to cast out a particular demon, he responded, "This kind cannot be driven out by anything but prayer and fasting" (Mark 9:29). In this same account in Matthew's Gospel Jesus responds that they were not able to cast out the demon because of their little faith (17:19). When we pray, we connect ourselves more tightly to God and are protected from demonic influence. When we fast, we create a physical emptiness in ourselves and come to realize that only God can satisfy the deepest longings of the human heart.

+ **Call upon your Guardian Angel** and remember your Guardian Angel is more powerful than the devil himself. Scripture teaches us the importance of our angels. In Psalm 91 [90] we read, "For he will give his angels charge of you to guard you in all your ways" (v. 11).

In Matthew's Gospel, Jesus says, "See that you do not despise one of these little ones; for I tell you that in heaven their angels always behold the face of my Father who is in heaven" (18:10). St. Bonaventure, a doctor of the Church (AD 1221–1274), sourced from Scripture a list of twelve ways that our Guardian Angels watch over us:

1. Rebukes us for our faults
2. Absolves us from the bonds of our sins
3. Takes away from us those things that impede goodness
4. Constrains the demons afflicting us
5. Teaches us
6. Reveals secrets about the mystery of God
7. Consoles us
8. Comforts us
9. Guides us and conducts us to God
10. Casts down our enemies
11. Mitigates our temptations
12. Prays for us and carries our prayers to God.

I believe our Guardian Angels are important because they serve to inspire us, instruct us, and illumine us to always be about the things of God.

+ **Use Sacramentals.** These are blessed objects and include things like scapulars, a crucifix, Miraculous

Medal, holy water, salt, and oil. The Code of Canon Law defines sacramentals as "sacred signs by which effects, especially spiritual effects, are signified in some imitation of the sacraments and are obtained through the intercession of the Church" (Can. 1166). The Catechism of the Catholic Church further adds that sacramentals "prepare us to receive grace and dispose us to cooperate with it" (1670). In the Acts of the Apostles there is an account of a deliverance that takes place through blessed objects: "And God did extraordinary miracles by the hands of Paul, so that handkerchiefs or aprons were carried away from his body to the sick, and diseases left them and the evil spirits came out of them" (19:11–12). Sacramentals are important because they always point us to Christ.

The Victory Belongs to Christ

Many people have remarked to me that they are surprised that I speak openly about the ministry of exorcism. There was a time in the Church when the identity of the exorcist was always kept secret. This is still the case for many exorcists throughout the world. Some do not want their identity to be known so as not to be inundated with callers. Their choice should be respected.

I have chosen to publicize my identity to better educate people about this important ministry. Talking about the ministry takes the mystique away from the practice of exorcism and allows people to know that they should not be afraid to approach the Church if they feel that something demonic is taking place in their lives. The Church exists as a vehicle to defeat the devil, as we make our journey to the tree of life. As more and more people are walking away from their Christian roots, or merely wearing the label of being a Christian, they are falling into the clutches of the devil. Therefore, it is more important than ever that the Church, through the ministry of exorcism, must stand ready to help these people overcome what the devil is doing to them and bring them to a true and genuine union with Jesus Christ.

It is my hope that what I have shared in these pages will not increase one's fear of Satan, but rather help people come to a deeper understanding of the saving power of Jesus Christ, who came to defeat the devil. Through his ordinary and extraordinary activities, the devil wants to destroy us and take our life away from us. In John's Gospel, Jesus says, "I came that they might have life, and have it abundantly" (10:10). In order to have this abundant life, that the devil wants to steal from us, I cannot stress enough the importance of actively living our faith. A lived and authentic relationship with Jesus Christ will always keep the devil at bay.

Recognizing the power of prayer, be assured of my thoughts and prayers for all of you. Please pray for me and all priests throughout the world who have been called to the ministry of exorcism. Your prayers mean more than you may ever know. Pray also for those afflicted by evil throughout the world who are seeking to be set free. Exorcism achieves this, for it is a powerful weapon that Jesus has placed in the hands of the Church to do battle against Satan and his angels.

PRAYERS

OUR FATHER

Our Father, who art in heaven, hallowed be thy name; thy kingdom come, thy will be done on earth, as it is in heaven. Give us this day our daily bread; and forgive us our trespasses as we forgive those who trespass against us; and lead us not into temptation, but deliver us from evil. Amen.

HAIL MARY

Hail Mary, full of grace, the Lord is with thee; blessed art thou among women, and blessed is the fruit of thy womb, Jesus. Holy Mary, Mother of God, pray for us sinners, now and at the hour of our death. Amen.

MEMORARE

Remember O most gracious Virgin Mary, that never was it known that anyone who fled to thy protection, implored thy help, or sought thy intercession, was left unaided. Inspired by this confidence, I fly unto thee, O Virgin of virgins, my Mother. To thee do I come, before thee I stand, sinful and sorrowful. O Mother of the Word Incarnate, despise not my petitions, but in thy mercy, hear and answer me. Amen.

FATIMA PRAYER

O my Jesus, forgive us our sins, save us from the fires of hell, lead all souls to heaven, especially those who are in most need of thy mercy. *Our Lady of Fatima, pray for us.*

HAIL HOLY QUEEN

Hail, holy Queen, Mother of mercy, our life, our sweetness and our hope, to thee do we cry, poor banished children of Eve; to thee do we send up our sighs, mourning and weeping in this valley of tears; turn, then, most gracious Advocate, thine eyes of mercy toward us, and after this our exile, show unto us the blessed fruit of thy womb, Jesus. O clement, O loving, O sweet Virgin Mary! Pray for us, O holy Mother of God, that we may be made worthy of the promises of Christ. Amen.

Mary, Mother of Grace

Mary, Mother of Grace,
Mother of mercy,
shield me from the enemy
and receive me at the hour of my death. Amen.

St. Cyril of Alexandria, from a homily delivered at the Council of Ephesus (AD 431)

Mary, Mother of God, we salute you, Precious vessel, worthy of the whole world's reverence, you are an ever-shining light, the crown of virginity, the symbol of orthodoxy, an indestructible temple, the place that held him whom no place can contain, mother and virgin. Because of you the holy gospels could say: "Blessed is he who comes in the name of the Lord."

We salute you, for in your holy womb he, who is beyond all limitation was confined. Because of you the Holy Trinity is glorified and adored; the cross is called precious and is venerated throughout the world; the heavens exult; the angels and archangels make merry; demons are put to flight; the devil, that tempter, is thrust down from heaven; the fallen race of man is taken up on high; all creatures possessed by the madness of idolatry have attained knowledge of the truth; believers receive holy baptism; the oil of gladness is poured out; the Church is established throughout the world; pagans are brought to repentance.

St. Joseph, Terror of Demons

Saint Joseph, Terror of Demons, cast your solemn gaze upon the devil and all his minions, and protect us with your mighty staff. You fled through the night to avoid the devil's wicked designs; now with the power of God, smite the demons as they flee from you! Grant special protection, we pray, for children, fathers, families, and the dying. By God's grace, no demon dares approach while you are near, so we beg of you, always be near to us! Amen.

Psalm 3

O Lord, how many are my foes! Many are rising against me; many are saying of me, there is no help for him in God. But you, O Lord, are a shield about me, my glory, and the lifter of my head. I cry aloud to the Lord, and he answers me from his holy mountain. I lie down in sleep; I wake again, for the Lord sustains me. I am not afraid of ten thousands of people who have set themselves against me round about. Arise, O Lord! Deliver me, O my God! For you strike all my enemies on the cheek, you break the teeth of the wicked. Deliverance belongs to the Lord; your blessing be upon your people!

PSALM 31[30]:1–5

In you, O Lord, I seek refuge; let me never be put to shame; in your righteousness deliver me! Incline your ear to me, rescue me speedily! Be a rock of refuge for me, a strong fortress to save me! Yes, you are my rock and my fortress; for your name's sake lead me and guide me, take me out of the net which is hidden for me, for you are my refuge. Into your hand I commit my spirit; you have redeemed me, O Lord, faithful God.

PSALM 68[67]:1–2

Let God arise, let his enemies be scattered; let those who hate him flee before him! As smoke is driven away, so drive them away; as wax melts before fire, let the wicked perish before God!

PSALM 91[90]

He who dwells in the shelter of the Most High, who abides in the shadow of the Almighty, will say to the Lord, "My refuge and my fortress; my God, in whom I trust." For he will deliver you from the snare of the fowler and from the deadly pestilence; he will cover you with his pinions, and under his wings you will find refuge; his faithfulness is a shield and buckler. You will not fear the terror of the night, nor the arrow that flies by day, nor the pestilence that stalks in darkness, nor the destruction that wastes at noonday. A thousand may fall at your side, ten thousand at your right hand; but it will not come near you. You will only look with your eyes and see the recompense of the wicked. Because you have made the Lord your refuge, the Most High your habitation, no evil shall befall you, no scourge come near your tent. For he will give his angels charge of you to guard you in all your ways. On their hands they will bear you up, lest you dash your foot against a stone. You will tread on the lion and the adder, the young lion and the serpent you will trample under foot. Because he clings to me in love, I will deliver him; I will protect him, because he knows my name. When he calls to me, I will answer him; I will be with him in trouble, I will rescue him and honor him. With long life I will satisfy him, and show him my salvation.

St. Michael the Archangel Prayer

Saint Michael the Archangel, defend us in battle. Be our protection against the wickedness and snares of the devil. May God rebuke him, we humbly pray; and do thou, O Prince of the Heavenly Host—by the Divine Power of God—cast into hell Satan and all the evil spirits, who roam throughout the world seeking the ruin of souls. Amen.

Prayer to St. Michael

Glorious St. Michael, Prince of the heavenly hosts, who stands always ready to give assistance to the people of God; who didst fight with the dragon, the old serpent, and didst cast him out of heaven, and now valiantly defends the Church of God that the gates of hell may never prevail against her, I earnestly entreat thee to assist me also, in the painful and dangerous conflict which I have to sustain against the same formidable foe. Be with me, O mighty Prince! that I may courageously fight and wholly vanquish that proud spirit, whom thou hast by the Divine Power, so gloriously overthrown, and whom our powerful King, Jesus Christ, has, in our nature, so completely overcome; to the end that having triumphed over the enemy of my salvation, I may with thee and the holy angels, praise the clemency of God who, having refused mercy to the rebellious angels after their fall, has granted repentance and forgiveness to fallen man. Amen.

The Chaplet of St. Michael

O God, come to my assistance. O Lord, make haste to help me. Glory be to the Father, and to the Son, and to the Holy Spirit, as it was is the beginning is now and ever shall be, world without end. Amen.

(*Say one Our Father and three Hail Marys after each of the nine angelic invocations.*)

1. By the intercession of St. Michael and the celestial Choir of Seraphim may the Lord make us worthy to burn with the fire of perfect charity. Amen.

2. By the intercession of St. Michael and the celestial Choir of Cherubim may the Lord grant us the grace to leave the ways of sin and run in the paths of Christian perfection. Amen.

3. By the intercession of St. Michael and the celestial Choir of Thrones may the Lord infuse into our hearts a true and sincere spirit of humility. Amen.

4. By the intercession of St. Michael and the celestial Choir of Dominations may the Lord give us grace to govern our senses and overcome any unruly passions. Amen.

5. By the intercession of St. Michael and the celestial Choir of Virtues may the Lord preserve us from evil and falling into temptation. Amen.

6. By the intercession of St. Michael and the celestial Choir of Powers may the Lord protect our souls against the snares and temptations of the devil. Amen.

7. By the intercession of St. Michael and the celestial Choir of Principalities may God fill our souls with a true spirit of obedience. Amen.

8. By the intercession of St. Michael and the celestial Choir of Archangels may the Lord give us perseverance in faith and in all good works in order that we may attain the glory of Heaven. Amen.

9. By the intercession of St. Michael and the celestial Choir of Angels may the Lord grant us to be protected by them in this mortal life and conducted in the life to come to Heaven. Amen.

Say one Our Father in honor of each of the following angelic creatures: St. Michael, St. Gabriel, St. Raphael, and our Guardian Angel.

O glorious prince St. Michael, chief and commander of the heavenly hosts, guardian of souls, vanquisher of rebel spirits, servant in the house of the Divine King and our admirable conductor, you who shine with excellence and superhuman virtue, deliver us from all evil, who turn to you with confidence, and enable us by your gracious protection to serve God more and more faithfully every day. Pray for us, O glorious St. Michael, Prince of the Church of Jesus Christ, that we may be made worthy of His promises.

Almighty and Everlasting God, Who, by a prodigy of goodness and a merciful desire for the salvation of all men, has appointed the most glorious Archangel St. Michael Prince of Your Church, make us worthy, we ask You, to be delivered from all our enemies, that none of them may harass us at the hour of death, but that we may be conducted by him into Your Presence. This we ask through the merits of Jesus Christ Our Lord. Amen.

Prayer to St. Michael

O Prince of the heavenly host, Saint Michael, thou who cast into hell proud Lucifer with all his followers, thou who art defender and protector of the Church, thou who art protector of souls departing this world, come to the aid of the people of God and defend the Church committed unto thee against all the snares of Satan. Help my soul which I now commend to thee against this same enemy. Protect me especially at the hour of my death, so that I may be admitted to the joys of paradise where I, with all the angels, may praise God eternally. Amen.

Guardian Angel Prayer

Angel of God, my guardian dear, to whom his love commits me here, ever this day be at my side, to light and guard, to rule and guide. Amen.

St. Benedict

The Holy Cross be my light;
Let not the dragon be my guide.
Step back, Satan!
Never tempt me with your vanities.
What you offer me is evil.
Drink your own poison.

DIVINE PRAISES

Blessed be God.

Blessed be His Holy Name.

Blessed be Jesus Christ, true God and true man.

Blessed be the Name of Jesus.

Blessed be His most Sacred Heart.

Blessed be His most Precious Blood.

Blessed be Jesus in the Most Holy Sacrament of the Altar.

Blessed be the Holy Spirit, the Paraclete.

Blessed be the great Mother of God, Mary most holy.

Blessed be her Holy and Immaculate Conception.

Blessed be her glorious Assumption.

Blessed be the name of Mary, Virgin and Mother.

Blessed be Saint Joseph, her most chaste spouse.

Blessed be God in His Angels and in His Saints.

ST. JOHN CHRYSOSTOM'S DELIVERANCE PRAYER

O Eternal God, You who have redeemed the race of men from
the captivity of the Devil, deliver me, Your servant, from all
the workings of unclean spirits. Command the evil and im-
pure spirits and demons to depart from the soul and body
of Your servant and not to remain nor hide in me. Let them
be banished from me, the creation of Your hands, in Your
own holy name, and that of Your only-begotten Son, and of
Your life-creating Spirit, so that, after being cleaned from all

demonic influence, I may live godly, justly, and righteously and may be counted worthy to receive the Holy Mysteries of Your only-begotten Son and our God, with whom You are blessed and glorified, together with the all-holy and good and life-creating Spirit, now and forever and unto the ages of ages. Amen.

ANIMA CHRISTI

Soul of Christ, sanctify me; Body of Christ, save me; Blood of Christ, inebriate me; Water from the side of Christ, wash me; Passion of Christ, strengthen me; O good Jesus, hear me; within Your wounds, hide me; let me never be separated from You; from the evil one, defend me; at the hour of my death, call me; and bid me come to You; that with Your saints, I may praise You forever and ever. Amen.

PROTECTION PRAYER

Lord Jesus Christ be with me, defend me, be within me, conserve me; be before me that you may lead me; be after me that you may guard me; be above me that you may bless me, who with God the Father and the Holy Spirit lives and reigns forever and ever. Amen.

Renewal of Baptismal Promises

Do you reject Satan?

And all his works?

And all his empty promises?

Do you believe in God, the Father Almighty, creator of heaven and earth?

Do you believe in Jesus Christ, his only Son our Lord, who was born of the Virgin Mary, was crucified, died and was buried, rose from the dead, and is now seated at the right hand of the Father?

Do you believe in the Holy Spirit, the Holy Catholic Church, the Communion of Saints, the forgiveness of sins, the resurrection of the body, and life everlasting?

Selected Bibliography

Rituale Romanum: De Exorcismis Et Supplicationibus Quibus-dam. Editio Typica, apud Administrationem Patrimonii Sedis Apostolicae in Civitate Vaticana, 1999.

The Roman Ritual: Exorcisms and Related Supplications. English Translation According to the Typical Edition, For Use in the Diocese of the United States of America, Approved by the United States Conference of Catholic Bishops and Confirmed by the Apostolic See. Washington, DC: International Commission on English in the Liturgy Corporation, 2017.

USCCB Committee on Divine Worship, Frequently Asked Questions Regarding *Exorcisms and Related Supplications*, October 2014.

Amorth, Gabriele. *An Exorcist Explains the Demonic.* Translated by Charlotte J. Fasi. Manchester, NH: Sophia Institute Press, 2016.

Amorth, Gabriele. *Father Amorth: My Battle Against Satan.* With Elisabetta Fezzi. Translated by Charlotte J. Fasi. Manchester, NH: Sophia Institute Press, 2017.

Aquinas, Thomas. *Basic Writings of Saint Thomas Aquinas*, Volume One. Edited by Anton C. Pegis. Indianapolis/Cambridge: Hackett Publishing Company, 1997.

Bonino, Serge-Thomas, OP. *Angels and Demons: A Catholic Introduction.* Washington, DC: The Catholic University of America Press, 2016.

Cameli, Louis J. *The Devil You Don't Know: Recognizing and Resisting Evil in Everyday Life.* Notre Dame, IN: Ave Maria Press, 2011.

Cervinara, Tarcisio. *The Devil in the Life of Padre Pio.* San Giovanni Rotondo: Edizioni Padre Pio da Pietrelcina, 2009.

Collins, David, ed. *The Cambridge History of Magic and Witchcraft in the West.* Cambridge: University Press, 2015.

Daniélou, Jean. *The Angels and Their Mission.* Manchester, NH: Sophia Institute Press, 2009.

De Jesus-Marie, Bruno, OCD. *Satan.* New York, NY: Sheed & Ward, 1952.

Evagrius of Pontus. *Talking Back: A Monastic Handbook for Combating Demons.* Translated by David Brakke. Collegeville, MN: Liturgical Press, 2009.

Harris, Charles W., CSC. *Resist the Devil: A Pastoral Guide to Deliverance Prayer.* South Bend, IN: Greenlawn Press, 1988.

Lhermitte, Jean. *True or False Possession? How to Distinguish the Demonic from the Demented.* Manchester, NH: Sophia Institute Press, 2013 (Original work in English © 1963).

Nault, Jean-Charles, OSB. *The Noonday Devil: Acedia, the Unnamed Evil of Our Times.* San Francisco, CA: Ignatius Press, 2013.

Nortz, Fr. Basil, ORC. *Deliver Us From Evil.* Detroit, MI: Order of Canons Regular of the Holy Cross, 2000.

Suenens, Cardinal Léon-Joseph. *Renewal and the Powers of Darkness* (Malines Document IV). London: Darton, Longman and Todd, 1983.

Weller, Philip T., ed. and trans. *The Roman Ritual, Volume II: Christian Burial, Exorcism, Reserved Blessings, etc.* Boonville, NY: Preserving Christian Publications, Inc., 1952.